Arranged for Easy Piano by DAN COATES

Project Manager: CAROL CUELLAR
Art Design: KEN REHM

DAN COATES® is a registered trademark of Warner Bros. Publications

CONTENTS

THANK YOU

Words and Music by
DIDO ARMSTRONG
and PAUL HERMAN
Arranged by DAN COATES

Moderately slow (♩ = 80)

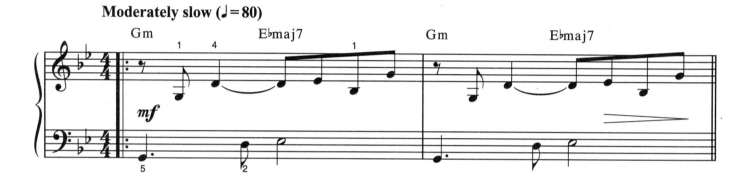

Verses 1 & 2:

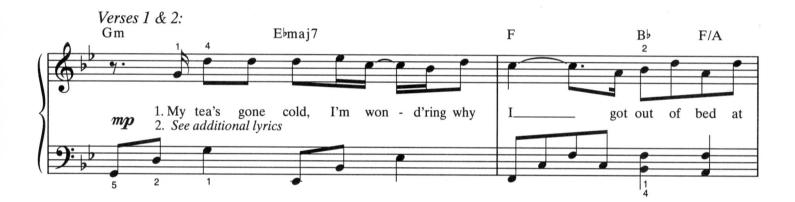

1. My tea's gone cold, I'm won-d'ring why I_____ got out of bed at
2. *See additional lyrics*

all. The morn-ing rain clouds up my win-dow and I can't see at

all. And e-ven if I could, it-'d all be grey, but your pic-ture on my

Thank You - 3 - 1

4

wall, it re - minds me that it's not so bad, it's not so bad.

2.

not so bad, it's not so bad.__ And

Chorus:

I__ want to

thank__ you__ for giv-ing me the best day__ of my

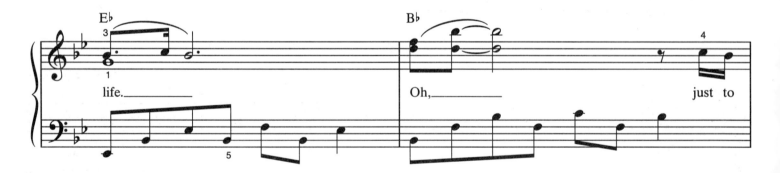

life.__ Oh,__ just to

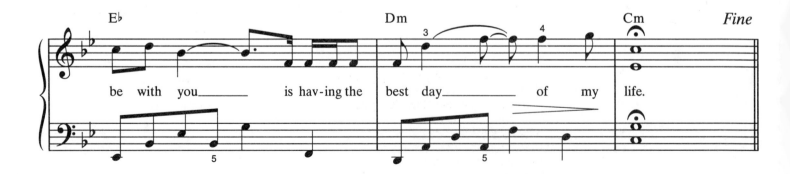

be with you__ is hav-ing the best day__ of my life.

Verse 3:

3. Push the door,___ I'm home at last___ and I'm soak - ing through___ and

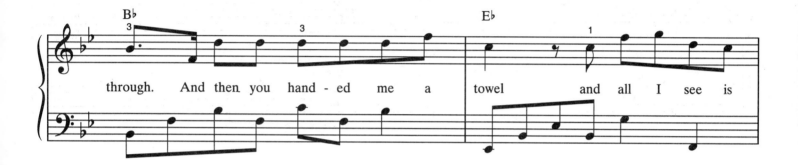

through. And then you hand - ed me a towel and all I see is

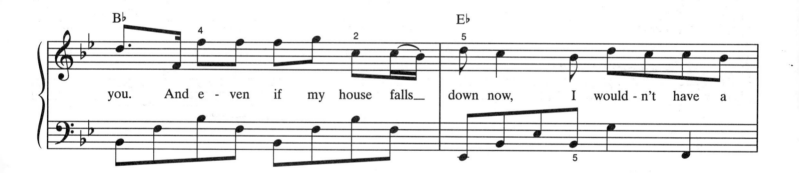

you. And e - ven if my house falls___ down now, I would - n't have a

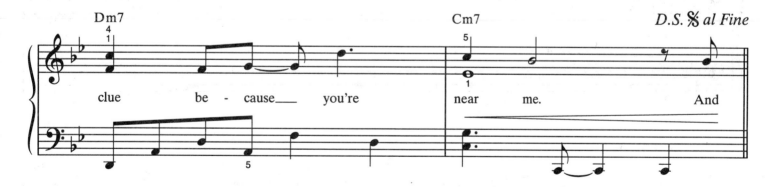

clue be - cause___ you're near me. And

Verse 2:
I drank too much last night, got bills to pay,
My head just feels in pain.
I missed the bus and there'll be hell today,
I'm late for work again.
And even if I'm there, they'll all imply
That I might not last the day.
And then you call me and it's not so bad, it's not so bad.
(To Chorus:)

NOBODY WANTS TO BE LONELY

Words and Music by
DESMOND CHILD, VICTORIA SHAW
and GARY BURR
Arranged by DAN COATES

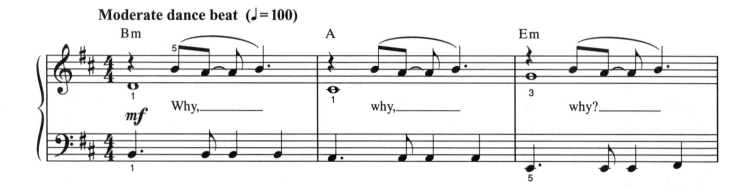

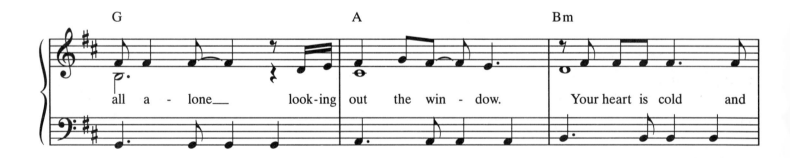

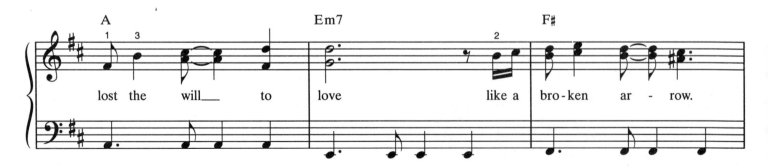

Nobody Wants to Be Lonely - 4 - 1

Here I stand in the shad-ows;_____ come to me, come to

cresc.

Chorus:

me, can't you see that No-bod-y wants___ to be lone-ly,

mf

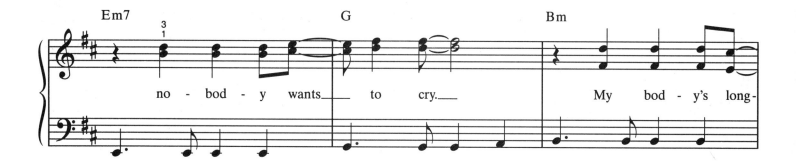

no-bod-y wants___ to cry.___ My bod-y's long-

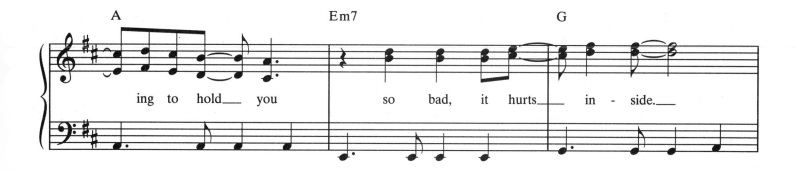

ing to hold___ you so bad, it hurts___ in-side.___

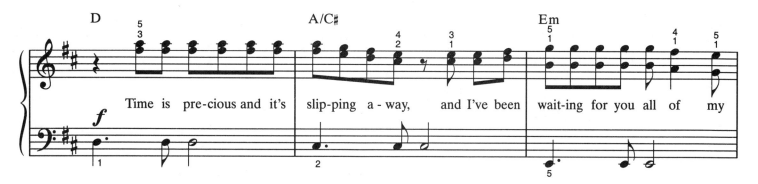

Time is pre-cious and it's slip-ping a-way, and I've been wait-ing for you all of my

f

8

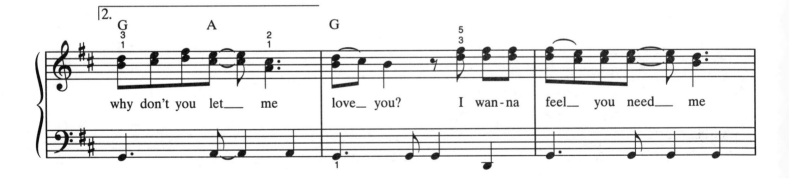

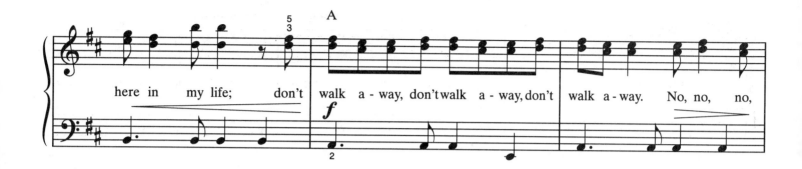

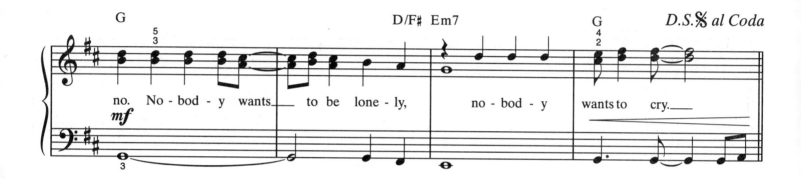

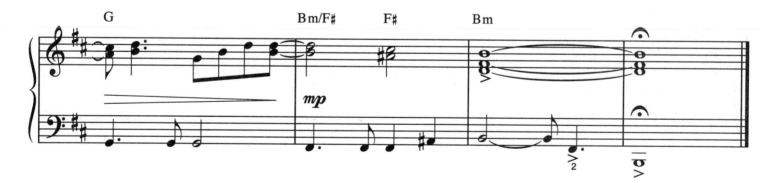

Verse 2:
Can you hear my voice?
Do you hear my song?
It's a serenade
So your heart can find me.
And suddenly you're flying down the stairs
Into my arms, baby.
Before I start going crazy,
Run to me, run to me
'Cause I'm dyin'.
(To Chorus:)

BREATHE

Words and Music by
STEPHANIE BENTLEY
and HOLLY LAMAR
Arranged by DAN COATES

Slowly (♩ = 60)

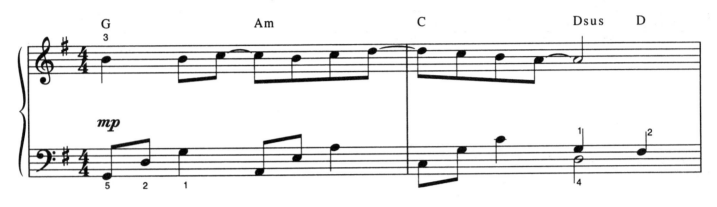

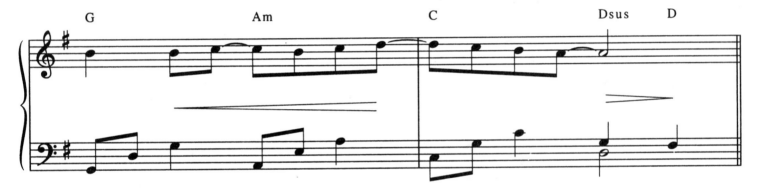

Verse 1:

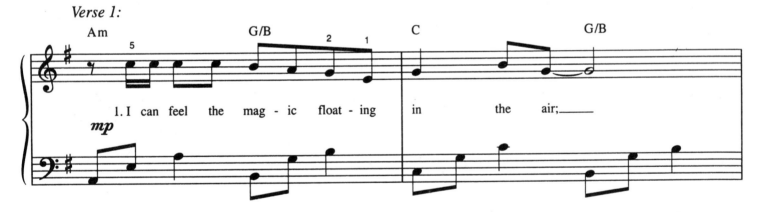

1. I can feel the mag - ic float - ing in the air;

be - ing with you gets me that way.

Breathe - 6 - 1

I watch the sun - light dance a - cross your face____ and I've

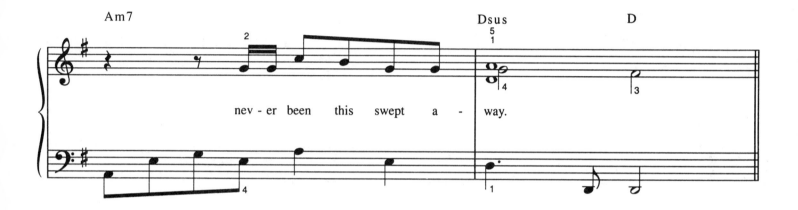

nev - er been this swept a - way.

Verses 2 & 3:

2. All my thoughts just seem to set - tle on the breeze____
3. In a way, I know my heart is wak - ing up____

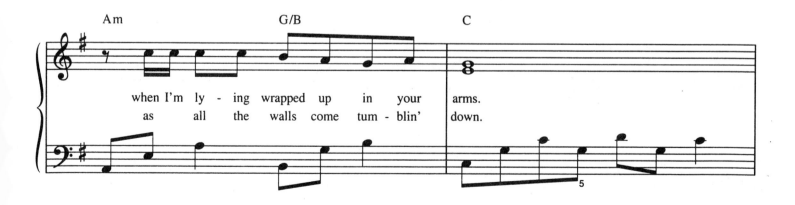

when I'm ly - ing wrapped up in your arms.
as all the walls come tum - blin' down.

12

The whole world just fades a - way, the on - ly thing____ I
Clos - er than I've ev - er felt be - fore and I know____ and you know

hear   is   the beat - ing   of   your heart._____   'Cause I can feel you
cresc.   there's no need for words right now._____

Chorus:

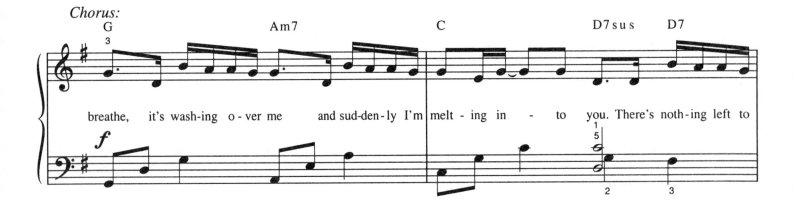

breathe, it's wash - ing o - ver me   and sud - den - ly I'm melt - ing in - to you. There's noth - ing left to
f

prove,   ba - by, all we need is just___ to be___   caught up in the

touch, the slow and stead-y rush. And, ba-by, is-n't that the way___ that love's sup-posed

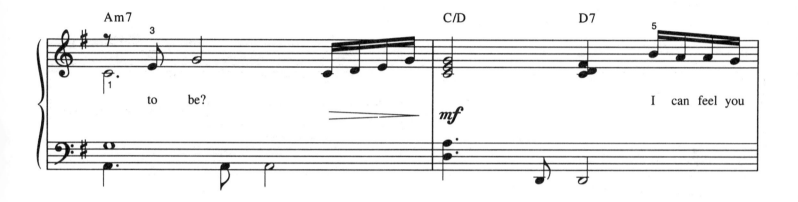

to be? *mf* I can feel you

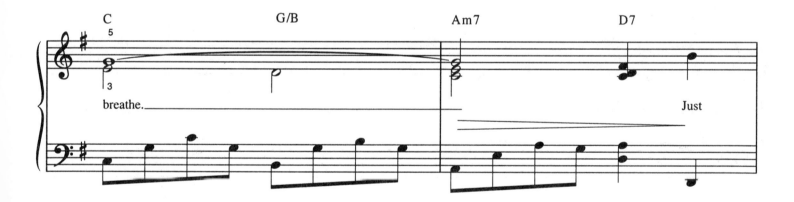

breathe._____ Just

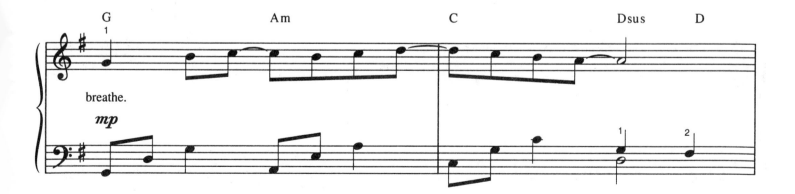

breathe. *mp*

14

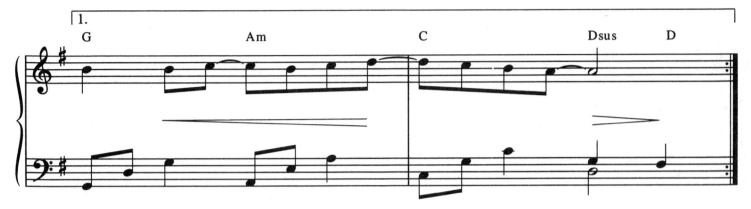

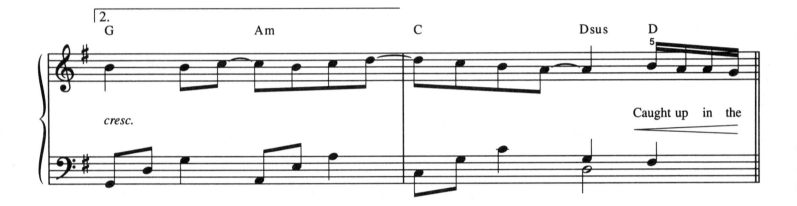

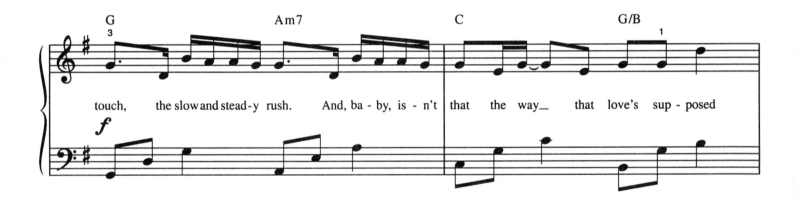

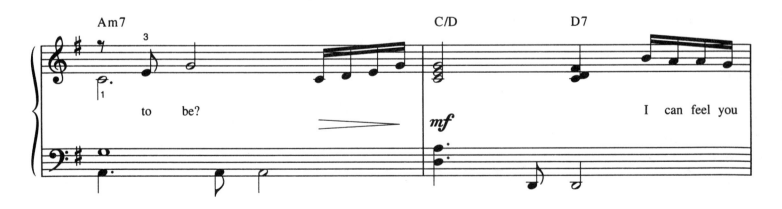

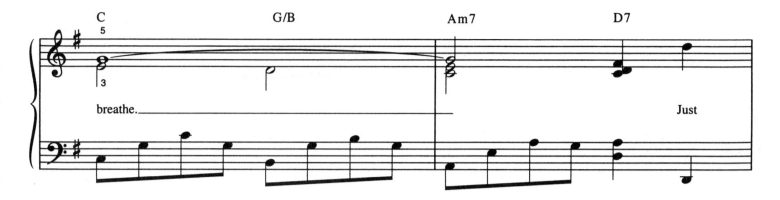

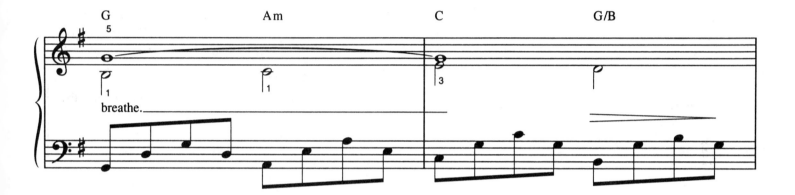

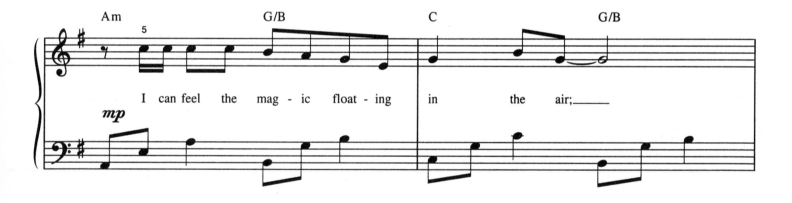

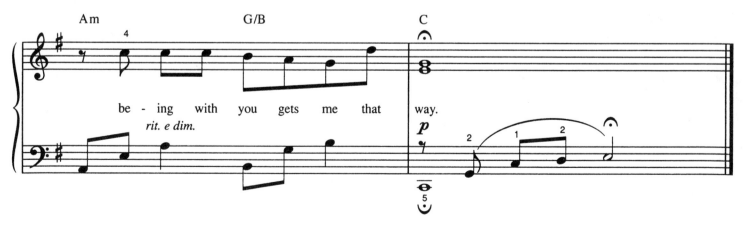

CAN'T FIGHT THE MOONLIGHT
(Theme from Coyote Ugly)

Words and Music by
DIANE WARREN
Arranged by DAN COATES

Moderate, steady beat (♩ = 98)

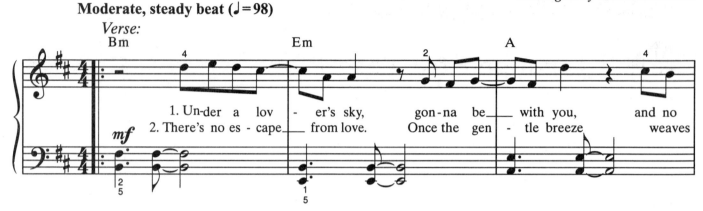

1. Un-der a lov-er's sky, gon-na be with you, and no
2. There's no es-cape from love. Once the gen-tle breeze

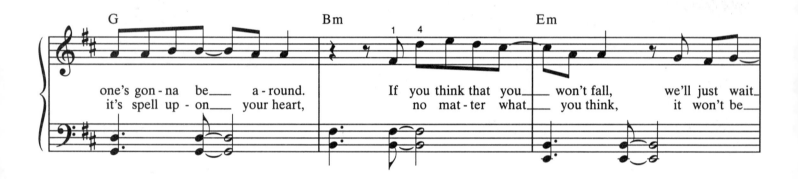

one's gon-na be a-round. If you think that you won't fall, we'll just wait
it's spell up-on your heart, no mat-ter what you think, it won't be

un-til, 'til the sun goes down. Un-der-neath the star-
too long 'til you're in my arms. Un-der-neath the star-

light, star-light, there's a mag-i-cal feel-ing so right.
light, star-light, we'll be lost in a rhy-thm so right.

Can't Fight the Moonlight - 4 - 1

Chorus:

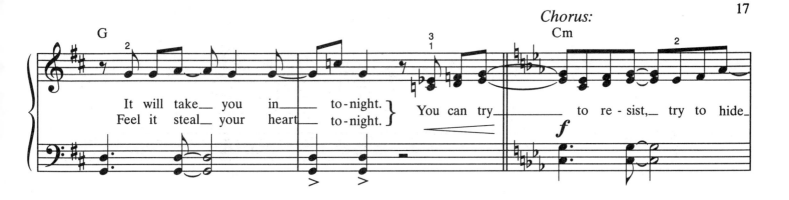

It will take_ you in_ to-night.
Feel it steal_ your heart_ to-night. You can try_ to re-sist, try to hide_

_ from my kiss,_ but you know, but you know_ that you can't fight the moon-light. Deep_

_ in the dark,_ you'll sur-ren - der your heart._ Don't you know,_ don't you know_ that you

1.

can't fight the moon-light, no, you can't fight_ it. It's

2.

gon-na get to your heart. no, you can't fight_ it._

18

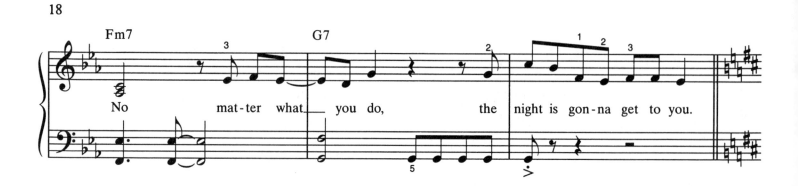

No mat-ter what you do, the night is gon-na get to you.

Bridge:

Can't fight it. Don't try it, you're

nev-er gon-na win, 'cause un-der-neath the star-light, star-light,

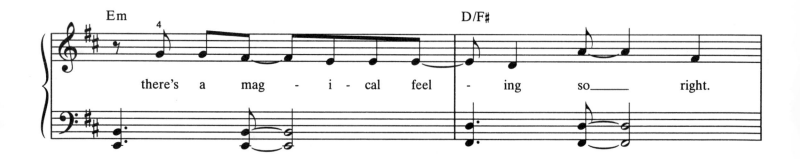

there's a mag-i-cal feel-ing so right.

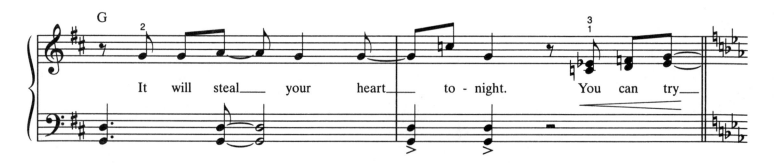

It will steal your heart to-night. You can try

Chorus:

COME ON OVER
(ALL I WANT IS YOU)

Words and Music by
PAUL REIN and JOHAN ABERG
Arranged by DAN COATES

Moderately fast (♩ = 120)

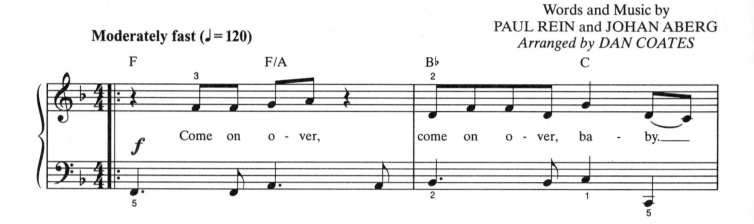

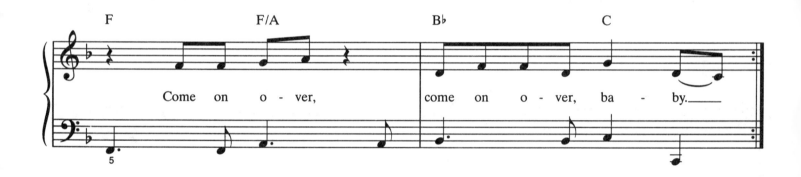

Verse:

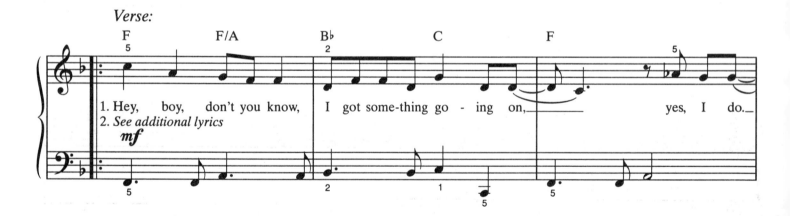

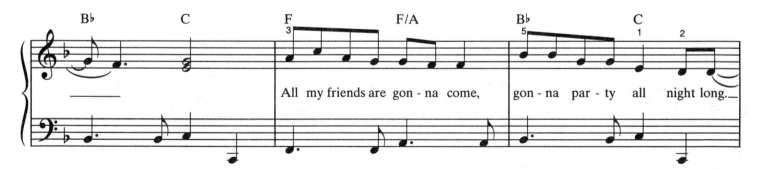

Come on Over - 4 - 1

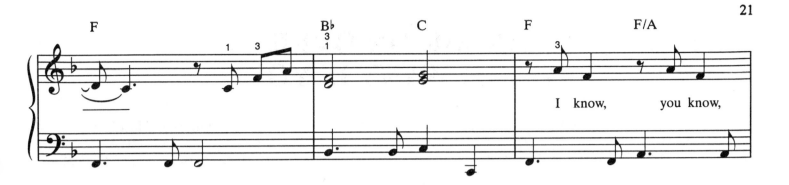

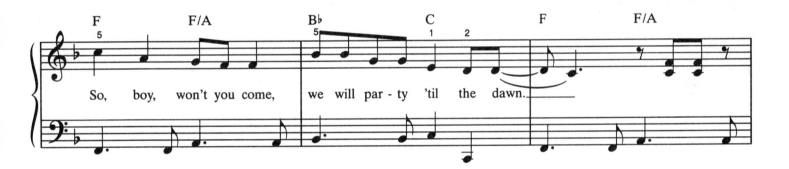

Chorus:

Come on Over - 4 - 2

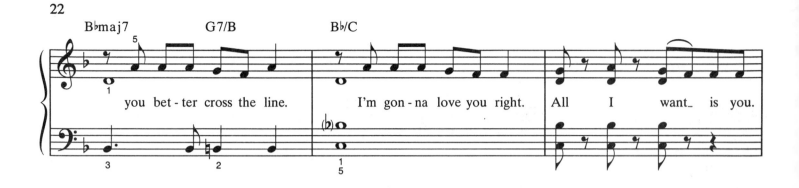

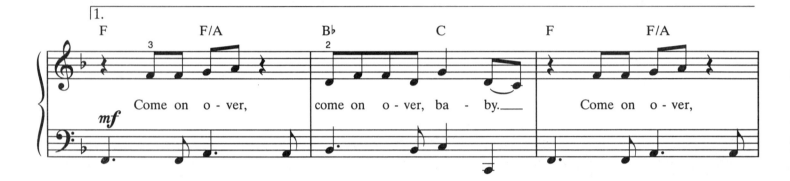

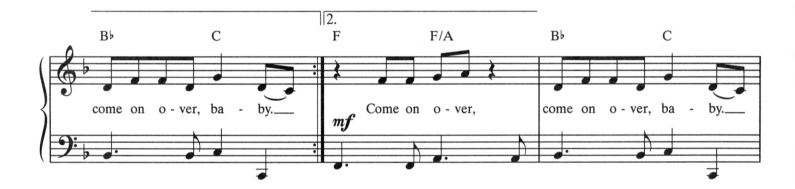

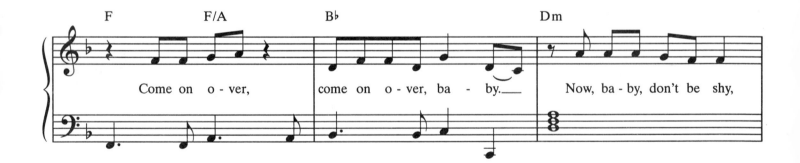

Chorus:

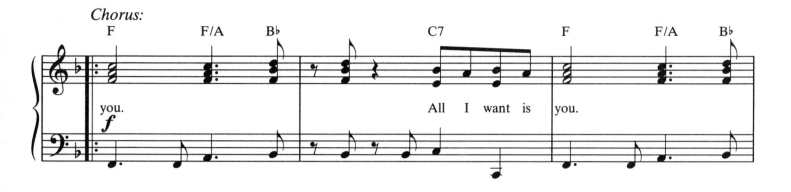

you. All I want is you.

All I want is you. Now, ba - by, don't be shy, you bet - ter cross the line.

I'm gon - na love you right 'cause all I, all I want is all I want is you.

Verse 2:
I want you to know,
You could be the one for me, yes, you could.
You've got all I'm looking for,
You've got personality.
I know, you know, I'm gonna give you more.
The things you do,
I've never felt this way before.
So, boy, won't you come,
Won't you come and open my door?
Listen to me.
(To Chorus:)

AMAZED

Words and Music by
MARV GREEN, AIMEE MAYO
and CHRIS LINDSEY
Arranged by DAN COATES

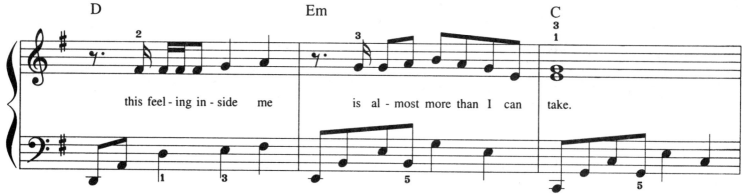

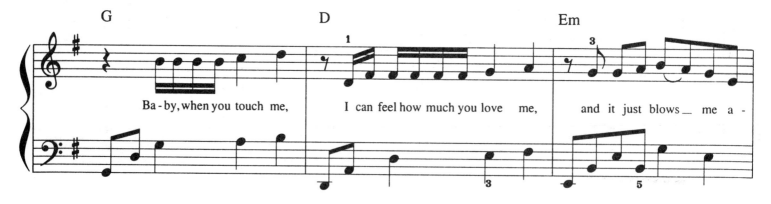

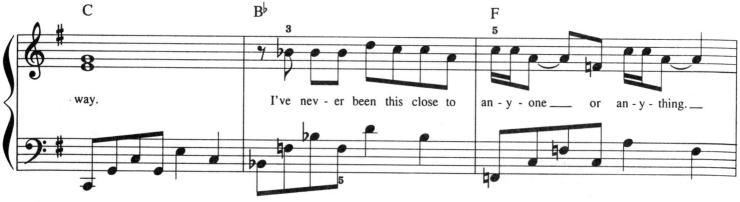

Amazed - 5 - 1

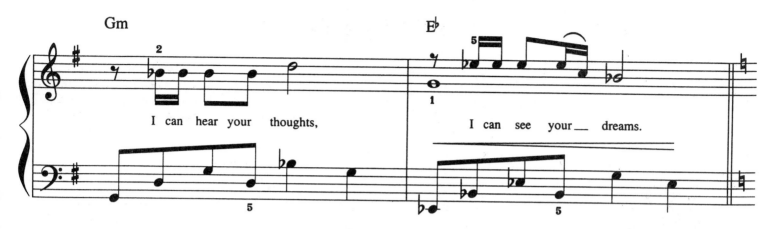

I can hear your thoughts,   I can see your___ dreams.

Chorus:

I don't know how you do what you do.___   I'm so in love with

you.   It just keeps get - ting bet - ter.

I wan - na spend the rest of my life___   with you by my side___

Amazed - 5 - 2

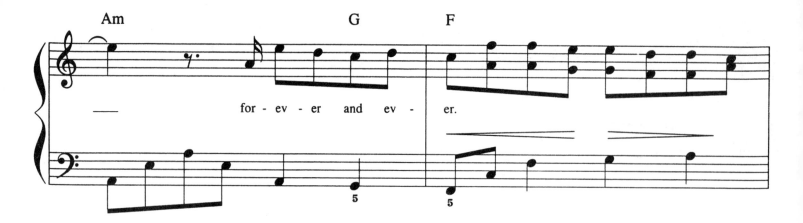

for - ev - er and ev - er.

Ev -'ry lit - tle thing that you do, ba - by, I'm a - mazed by

you. *dim.*

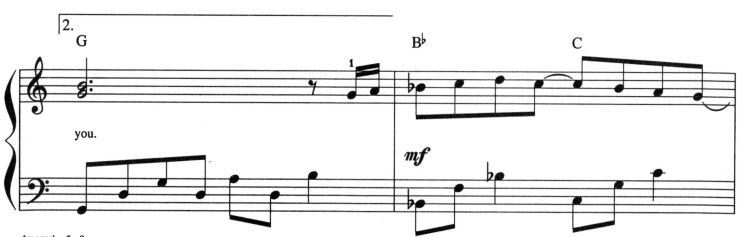

you.

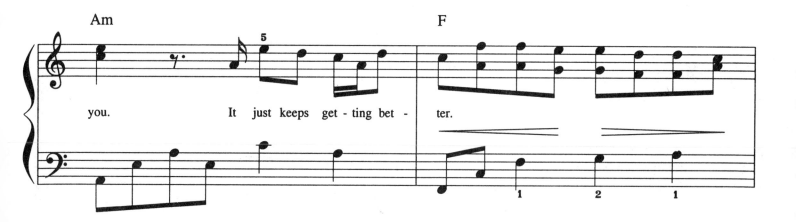

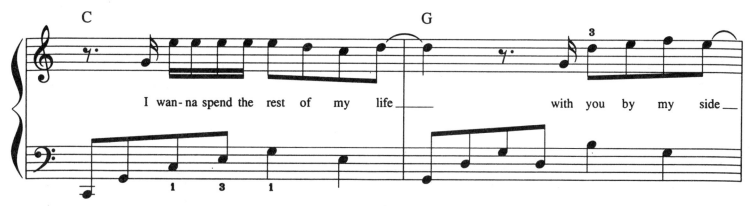

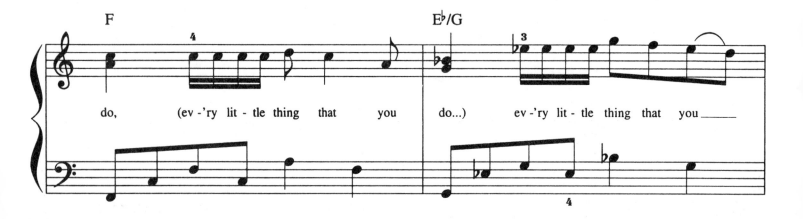

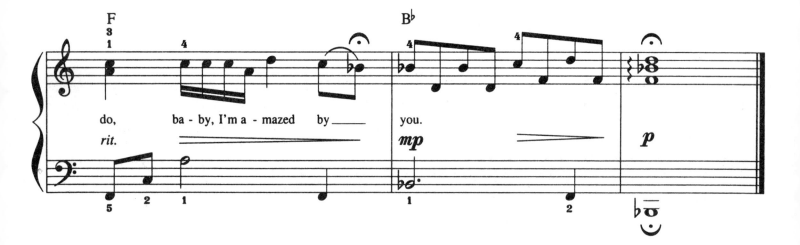

Verse 2:
The smell of your skin,
The taste of your kiss,
The way you whisper in the dark.
Your hair all around me,
Baby, you surround me.
You touch every place in my heart.
Oh, it feels like the first time every time.
I wanna spend the whole night in your eyes.
(To Chorus:)

DARE TO DREAM

Words and Music by
PAUL BEGAUD, VANESSA CORISH
and WAYNE TESTER
Arranged by DAN COATES

Moderately slow (♩ = 72)

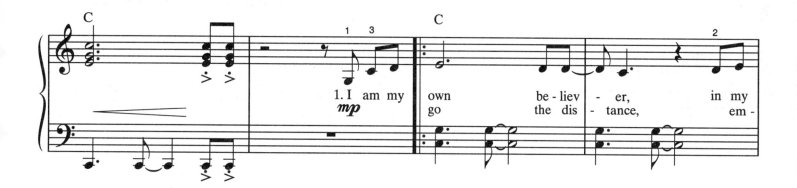

Dare to Dream - 5 - 1

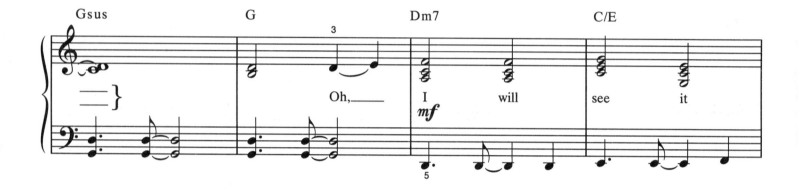

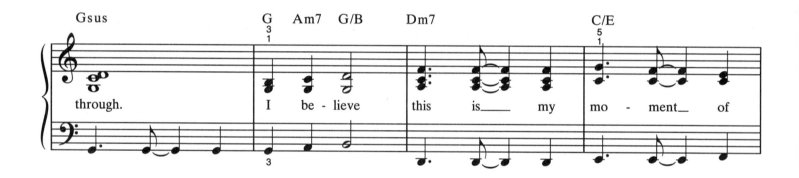

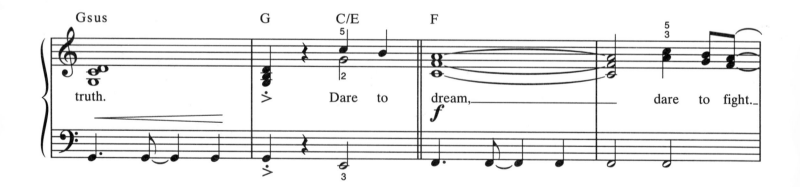

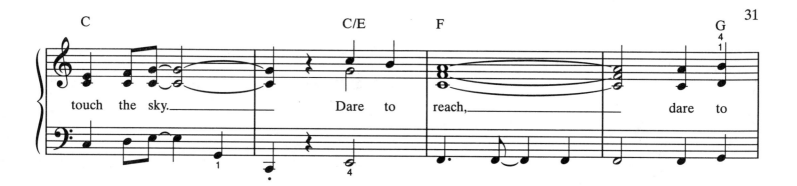

touch the sky._____ Dare to reach,_____ dare to

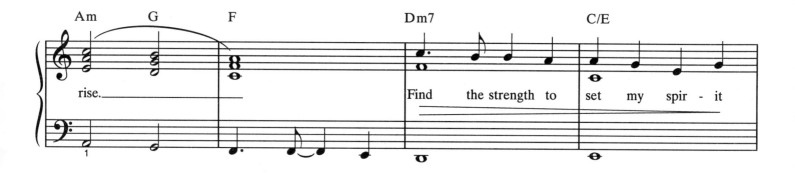

rise._____ Find the strength to set my spir - it

1.

free._____ Dare to dream.

mf

2.

2. I will free._____ Dare to

mp *mf*

dream. And my

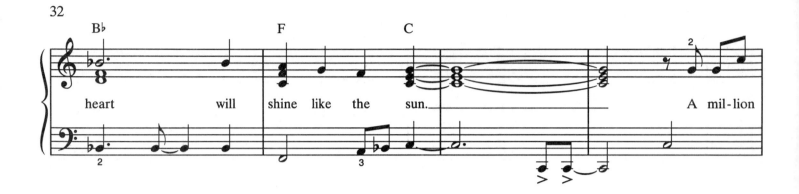
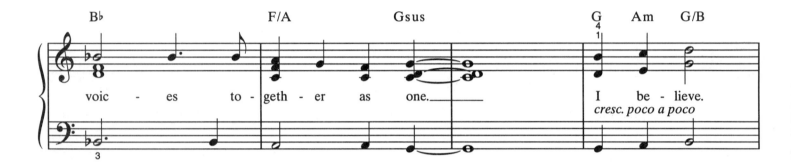
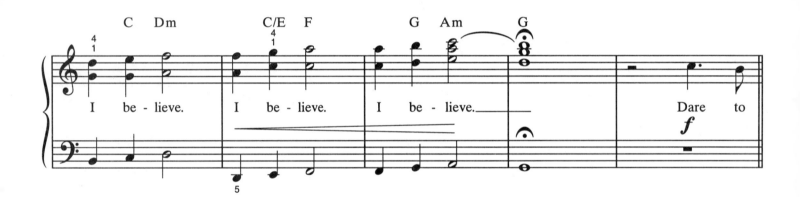

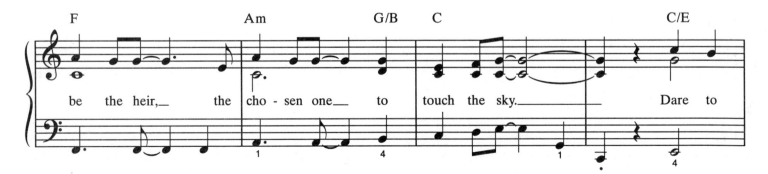

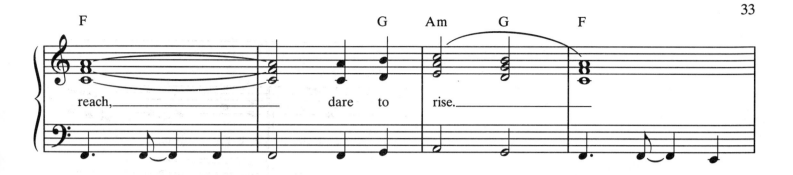

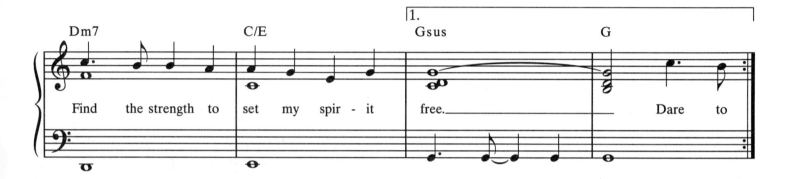

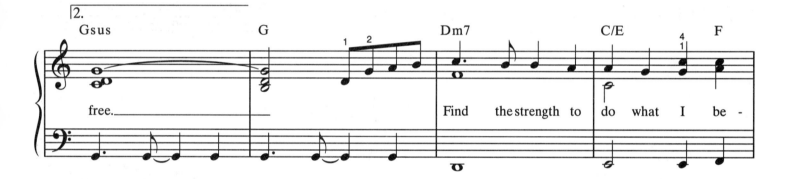

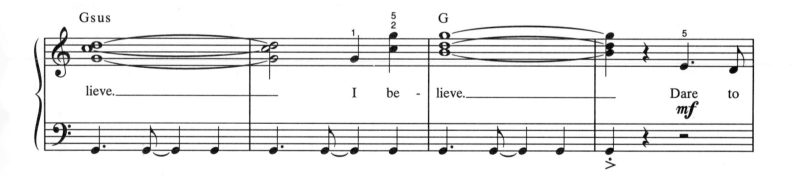

GIVE ME JUST ONE NIGHT
(UNA NOCHE)

Words and Music by
CLAUDIA OGALDE, ANDERS BAGGE
and ARNTHOR BIRGISSON
Arranged by DAN COATES

Moderately fast (♩ = 124)

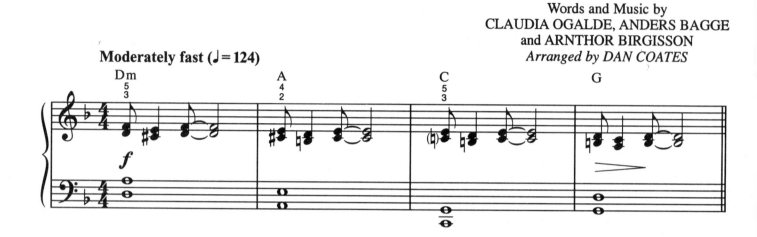

Verse 1:

1. Your lips keep tell-ing me you want me,_____ and hold me close all through the

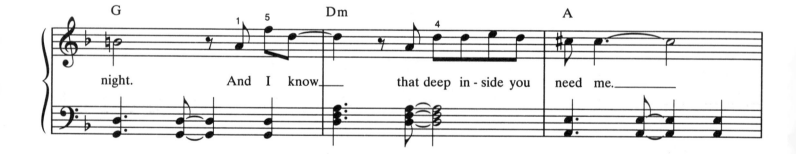

night. And I know___ that deep in-side you need me._____

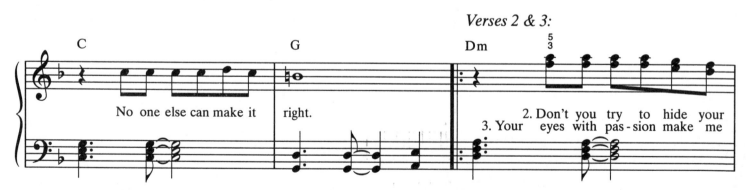

No one else can make it right.

Verses 2 & 3:

2. Don't you try to hide your
3. Your eyes with pas-sion make me

Give Me Just One Night - 3 - 1

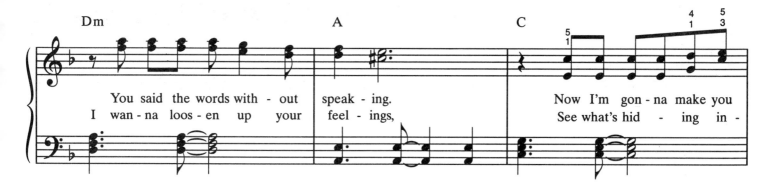

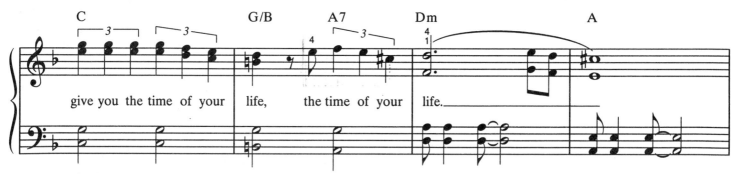

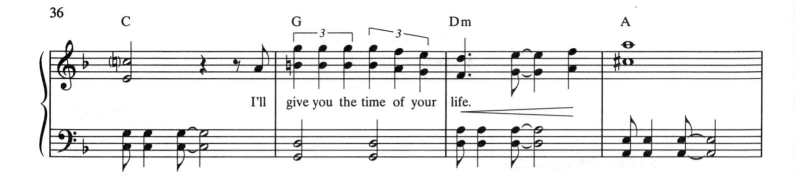

I'll give you the time of your life.

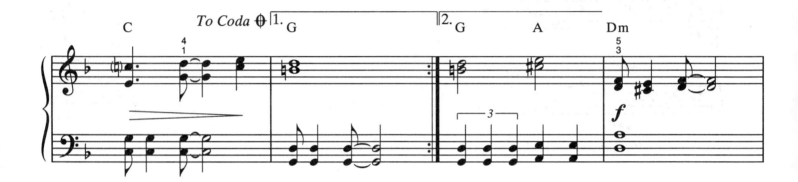

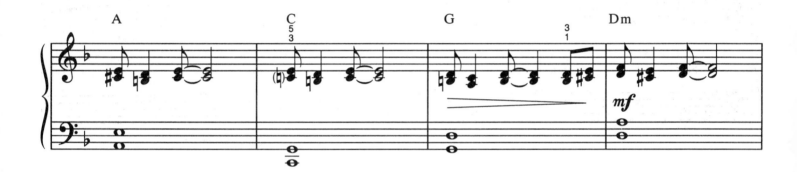

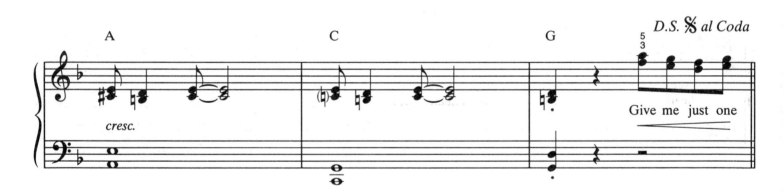

Give me just one

I BELIEVE

Words and Music by
ERIC LEVI
Arranged by DAN COATES

Slowly, with expression

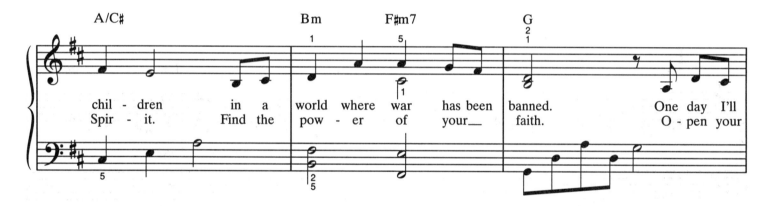

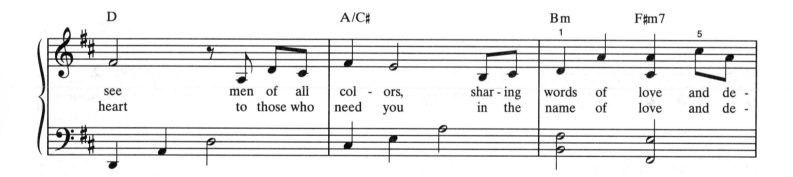

I Believe - 5 - 1

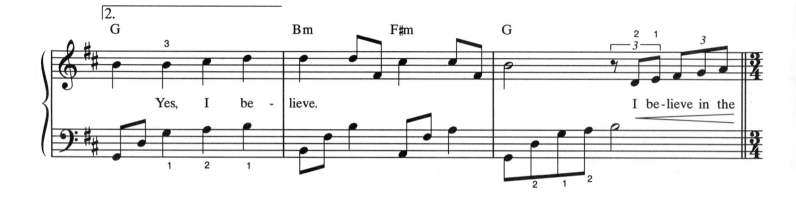

Yes, I be - lieve.

I be-lieve in the

Chorus:

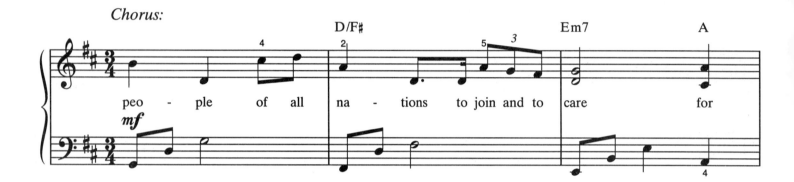

peo - ple of all na - tions to join and to care for

mf

love. I be-lieve in a world where light will guide us. And giv - ing our

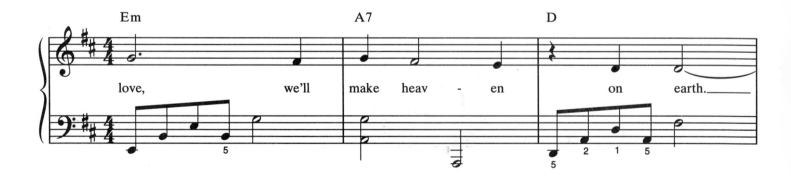

love, we'll make heav - en on earth.

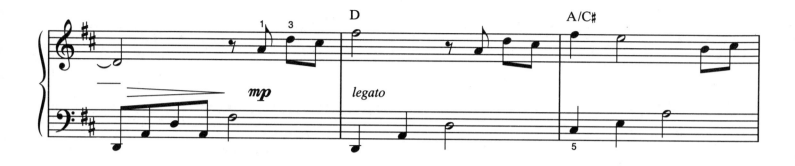

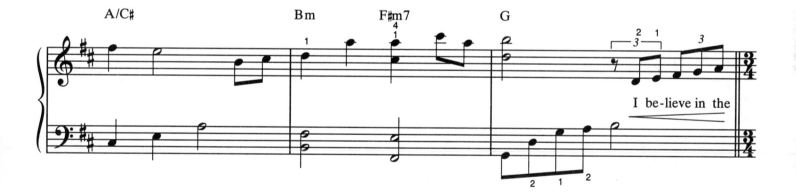

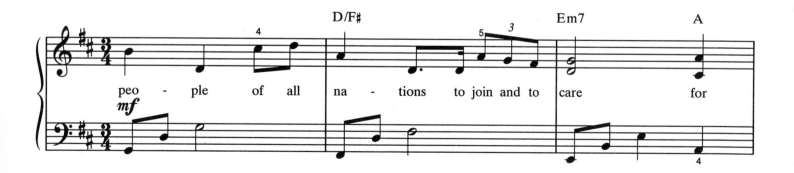

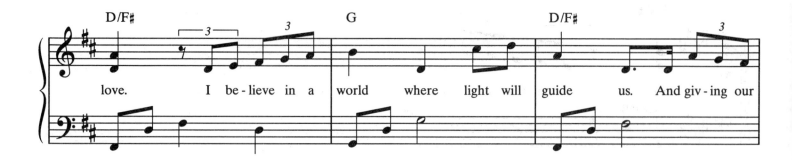

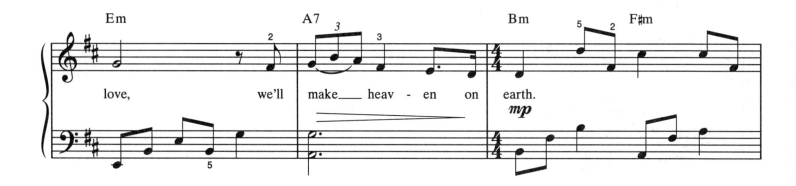

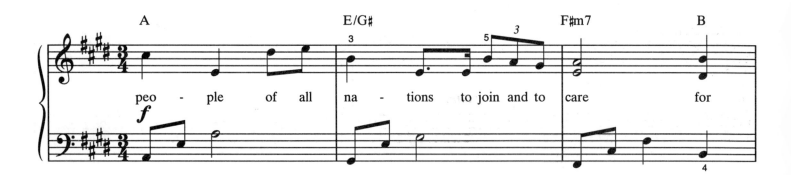

love.   I be - lieve in a   world,   and giv-ing our love   will make

heav - en on   earth.

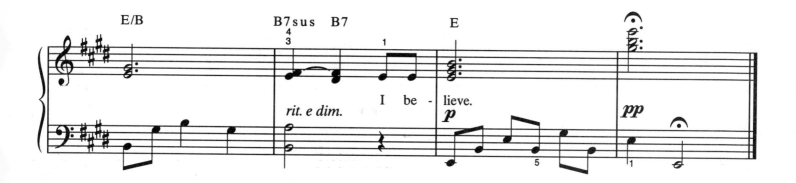

I be - lieve.

I HOPE YOU DANCE

Words and Music by
MARK D. SANDERS and TIA SILLERS
Arranged by DAN COATES

Moderately slow

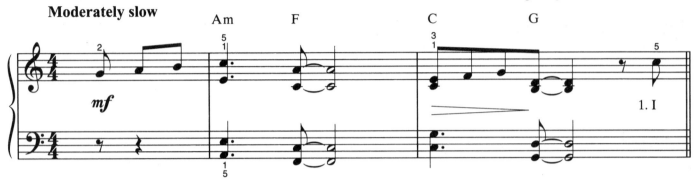

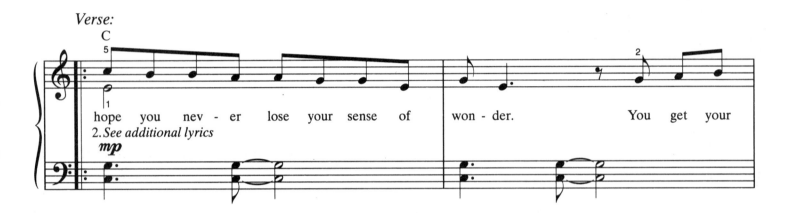

Verse:

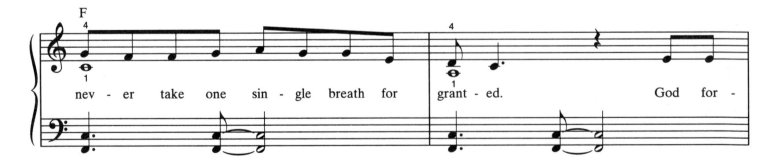

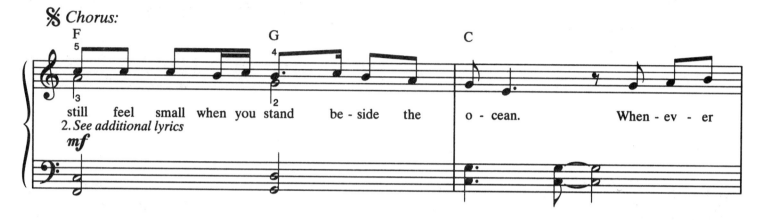

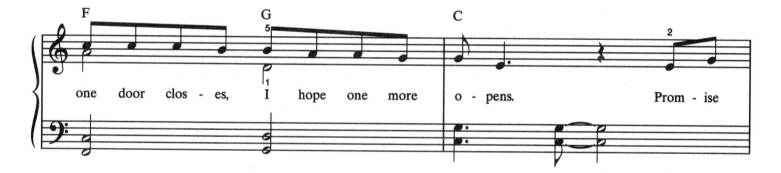

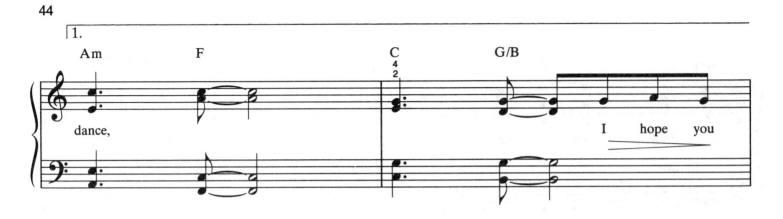

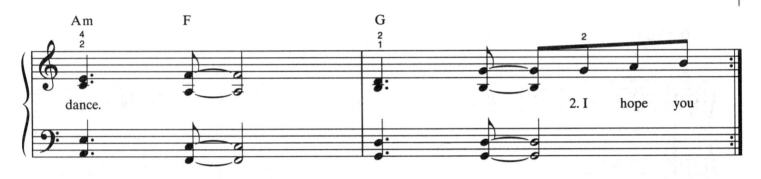

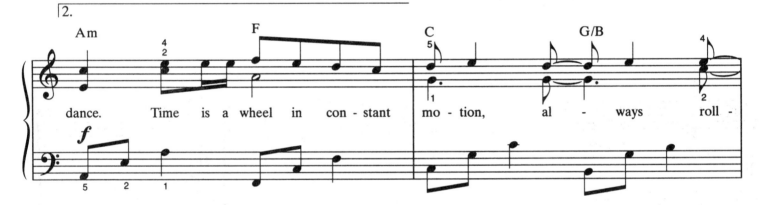

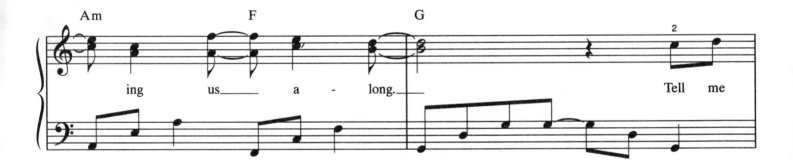

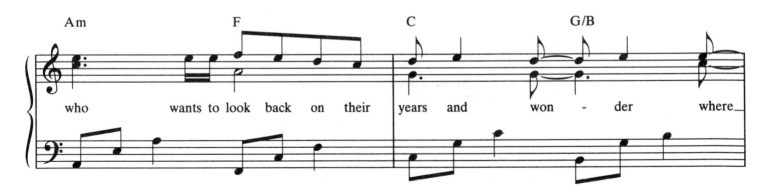

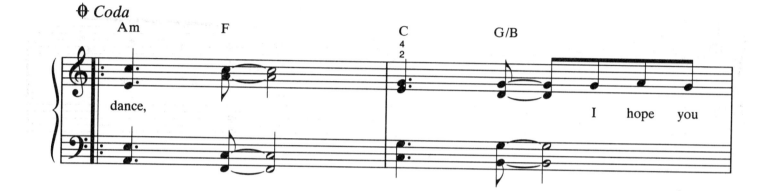

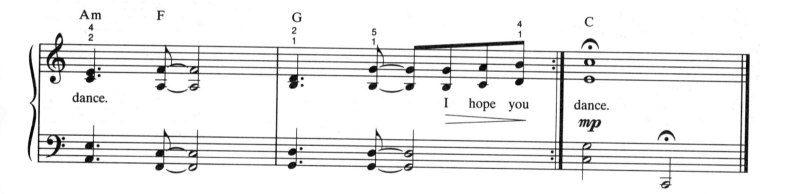

Verse 2:
I hope you never fear those mountains in the distance,
Never settle for the path of least resistance.
Livin' might mean takin' chances but they're worth takin'.
Lovin' might be a mistake but it's worth makin'.
(To Chorus 2:)

Chorus 2:
Don't let some hell-bent heart leave you bitter.
When you come close to sellin' out, reconsider.
Give the heavens above more than just a passing glance.
And when you get the choice to sit it out or dance,
I hope you dance.
(Repeat Chorus 1:)

I THINK I'M IN LOVE WITH YOU

Words and Music by
MARK ROONEY, DAN SHEA
and JOHN MELLENCAMP
Arranged by DAN COATES

Bright dance tempo (♩ = 106)

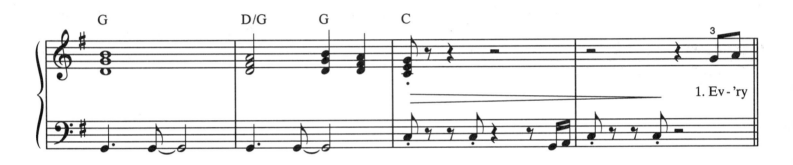

Verse:

time your near, baby, I get kind of cra-zy in my head for you___ and I don't know

2. *See additional lyrics*

what to do.___ And oh, ba-by, I get kind of shak-y when they

I Think I'm in Love With You - 4 - 1

men - tion you.___ I just lose my cool.___ My friends_ tell me

some - thing has come o - ver me and I think I know what it is.___ I think I'm in love.___

Chorus:

Boy, I think that I'm in love with you.___ Got me do - in' sil - ly things_ when it

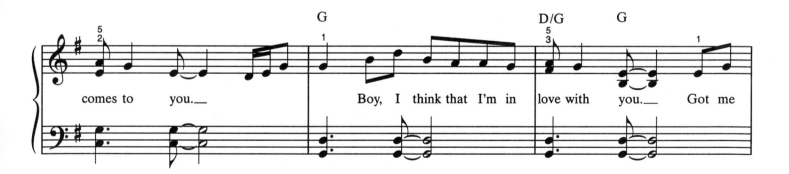

comes to you.___ Boy, I think that I'm in love with you.___ Got me

tell-in' all my friends what I feel for you. 2. Just the feel for you.

Some-thing strange has come o - ver me. Got me

go - in' out of my mind. Nev - er met a guy like you be - fore.

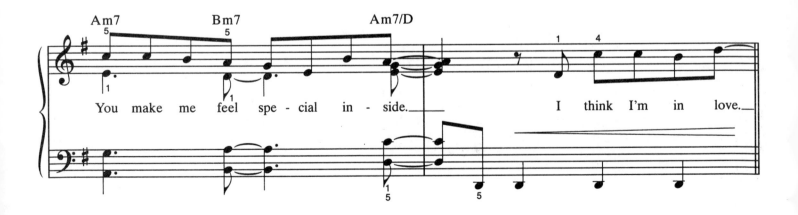

You make me feel spe - cial in - side. I think I'm in love.

G

Boy, I think that I'm in love with you.__ Got me do-in' sil-ly things__ when it

comes to you.__ Boy, I think that I'm in love with you.__ Got me

tell-in' all my friends__ what I feel for you.__ I'm in love.__ __

Verse 2:
Just the other night, baby,
I saw you hangin'.
You were with your crew.
I was with mine, too.
You took me by surprise
When you turned and looked me
In my eyes.
Oh, you really blew my mind.
I don't know what's gotten into me,
But I kinda think I know what it is.
I think I'm in love.
(To Chorus:)

IT'S MY LIFE

Words and Music by
JON BON JOVI, RICHIE SAMBORA
and MAX MARTIN
Arranged by DAN COATES

Steady rock beat (♩ = 120)

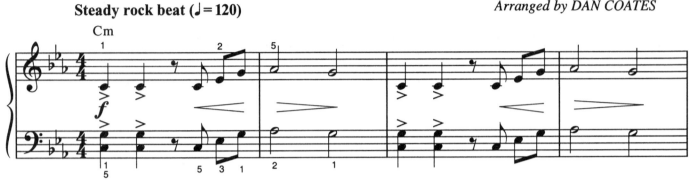

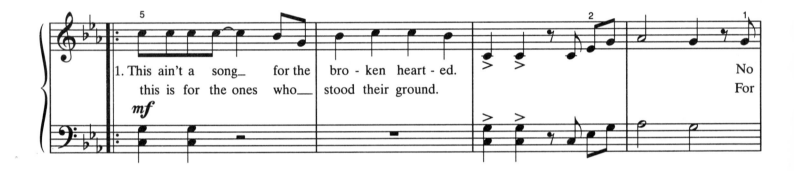

1. This ain't a song___ for the bro- ken heart- ed.
this is for the ones who___ stood their ground.

No
For

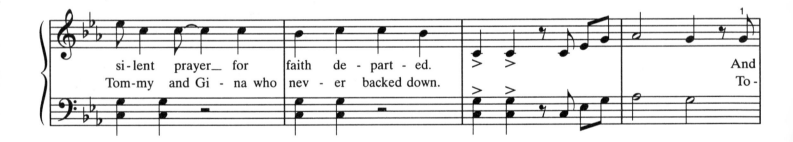

si- lent prayer___ for faith de- part- ed.
Tom- my and Gi- na who nev- er backed down.

And
To-

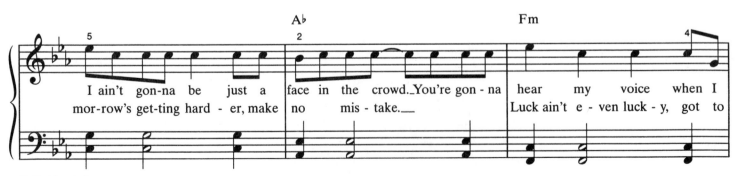

I ain't gon- na be just a face in the crowd. You're gon- na hear my voice when I
mor- row's get- ting hard- er, make no mis- take.___ Luck ain't e- ven luck- y, got to

It's My Life - 4 - 1

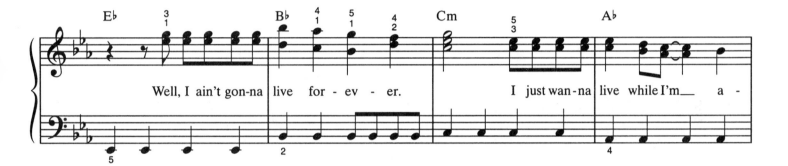

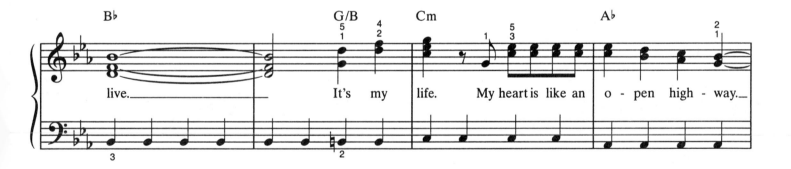

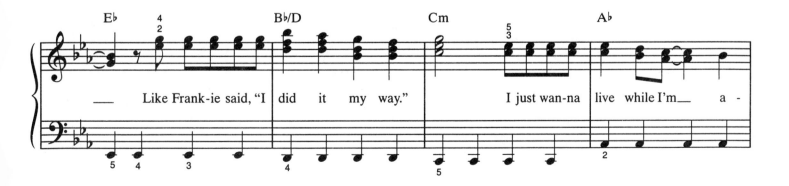

52

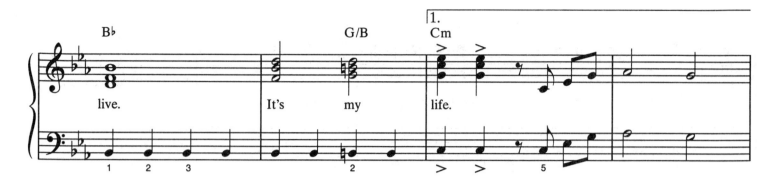

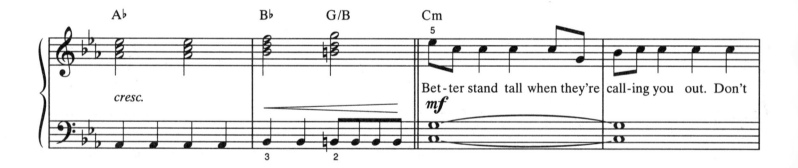

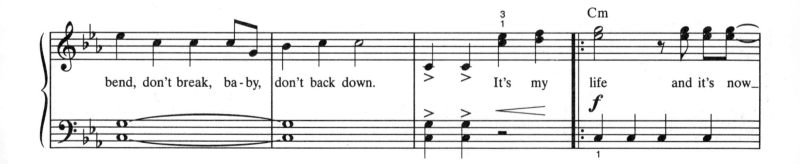

It's My Life - 4 - 3

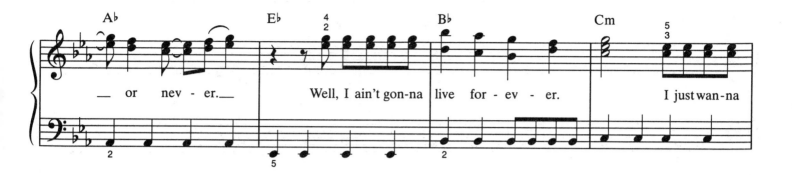

It's My Life - 4 - 4

I TURN TO YOU

Words and Music by
DIANE WARREN
Arranged by DAN COATES

Slowly (♩=76)

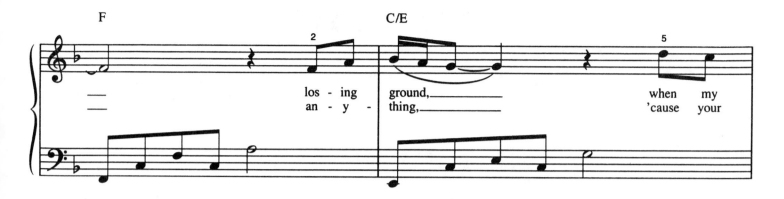

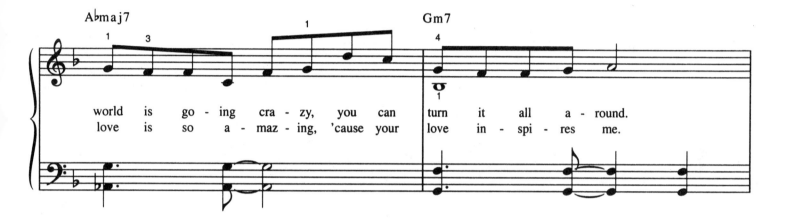

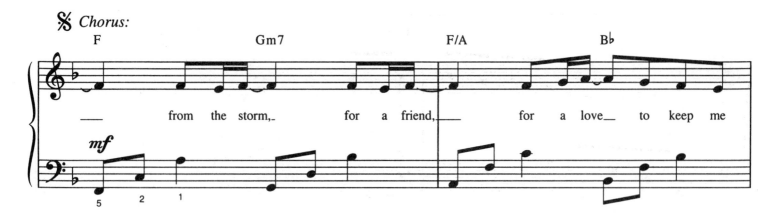

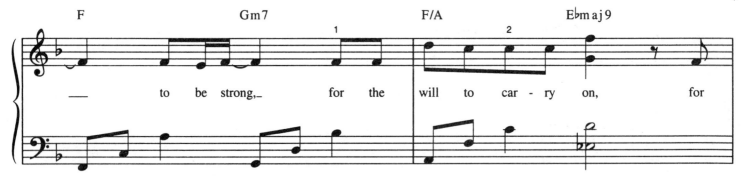

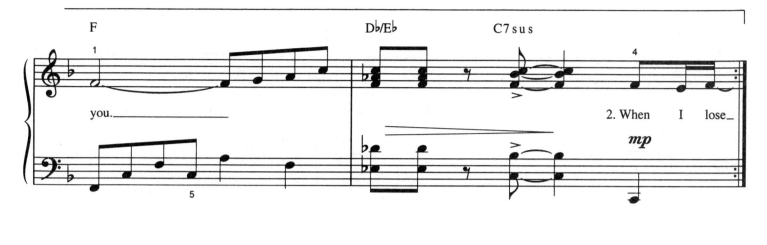

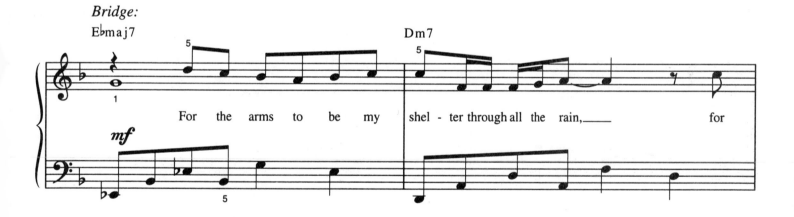

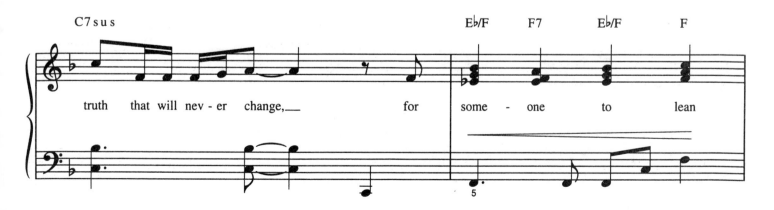

58

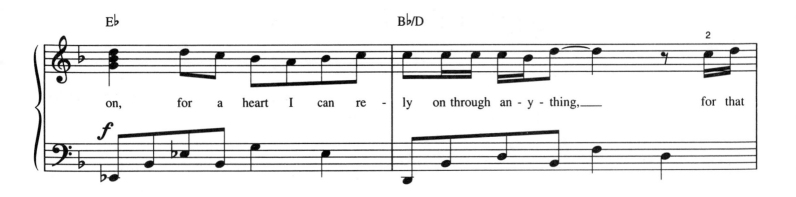

on,   for a heart I can re - ly on through an - y - thing,___   for that

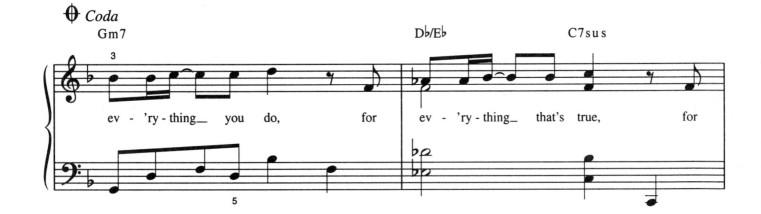

D.S. % al Coda

one   who___ I can run   to.   For a shield___

Coda
Gm7   Db/Eb   C7sus

ev - 'ry-thing___ you do,   for   ev - 'ry-thing___ that's true,   for

ev - 'ry-thing___ you do,   for   ev - 'ry-thing___ that's true, I turn to you.

THE LITTLE GIRL

Words and Music by
HARLEY ALLEN
Arranged by DAN COATES

Moderately slow ballad (♩ = 88)

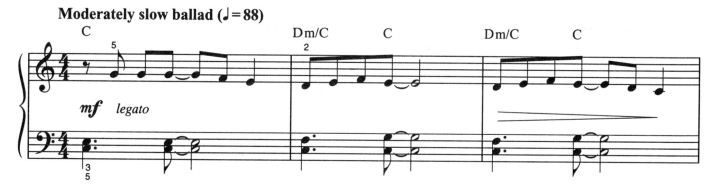

1. Her par-ents nev-er took the young girl to church,_ nev-er

spoke of His name,_ nev-er read her His word._ Two non-be-liev-ers walk-ing

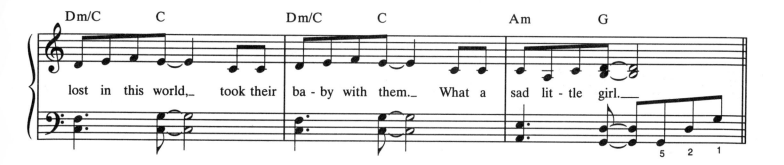

lost in this world,_ took their ba-by with them._ What a sad lit-tle girl.___

The Little Girl - 3 - 1

60

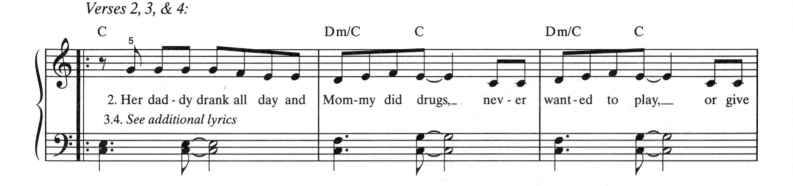

Verses 2, 3, & 4:

2. Her dad - dy drank all day and Mom - my did drugs,__ nev - er want - ed to play,__ or give
3.4. *See additional lyrics*

kiss - es and hugs.__ She'd watch the T V and sit there on the couch,__ while her

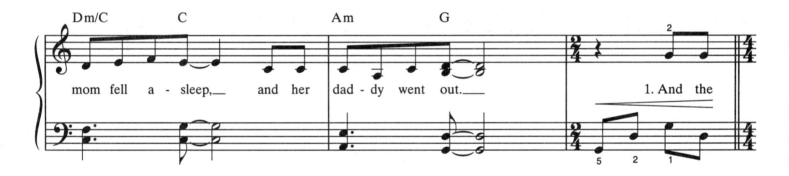

mom fell a - sleep,__ and her dad - dy went out.__ 1. And the

Chorus:

drink - ing__ and the fight - ing__ just got worse__ ev - 'ry night.__
2.3. *See additional lyrics*

Be - hind their couch__ she'd be hid - ing.__

The Little Girl - 3 - 2

Oh, what a sad lit-tle life.

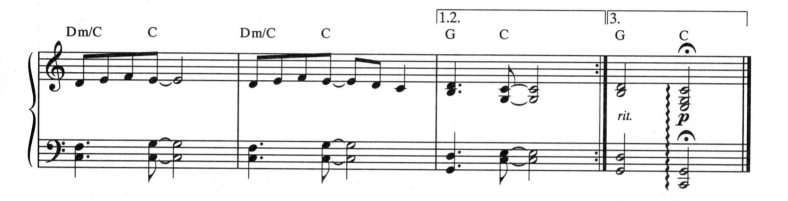

Verse 3:
And like it always does, the bad just got worse,
With every slap and every curse.
Until her daddy, in a drunk rage one night,
Used a gun on her mom and then took his life.

Chorus 2:
And some people from the city
Took the girl far away
To a new mom and a new dad,
Kisses and hugs every day.

Verse 4:
Her first day of Sunday school, the teacher walked in,
And a small little girl stared at a picture of Him.
She said, "I know that man up there on that cross.
I don't know his name, but I know he got off."

Chorus 3:
"'Cause He was there in my old house
And held me close to His side
As I hid there behind our couch
The night that my parents died."

LUCKY

Words and Music by
MAX MARTIN, RAMI
and ALEXANDER KRONLUND
Arranged by DAN COATES

Moderate, steady beat (♩ = 96)

Verse 1:

1. Ear - ly morn-ing, she wakes up. Knock, knock, knock on the door.

It's time for make-up, per-fect smile. It's you they're all wait-ing for. They go,

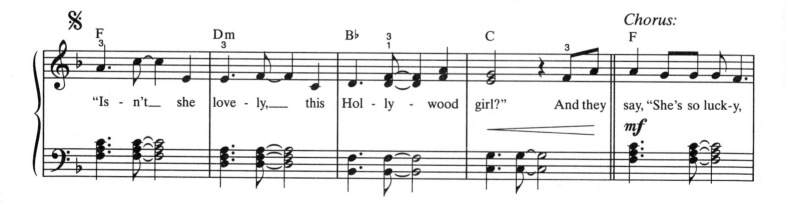

"Is - n't_ she love - ly,_ this Hol - ly - wood girl?" And they say, "She's so luck-y,

Chorus:

Lucky - 4 - 1

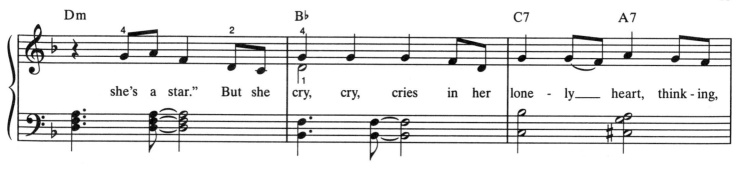

she's a star." But she cry, cry, cries in her lone - ly___ heart, think - ing,

if there's noth - ing miss - ing in my life, then why do___ these

To Coda ⊕ *Verse 2:*

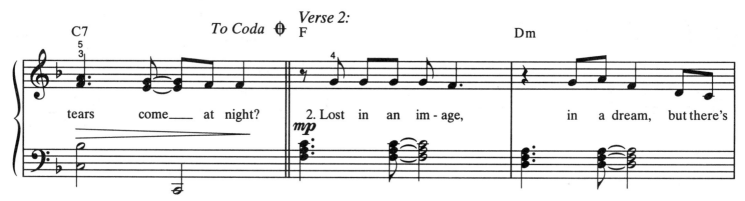

tears come___ at night? 2. Lost in an im - age, in a dream, but there's

no one there to wake her up. And the world is spin - ning and she

D.S. 𝄋 al Coda

C7   Dm

keeps on win - ning, but tell me, what hap - pens when it stops? They go,

64

Coda

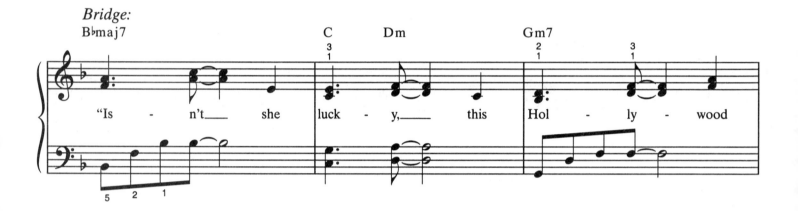

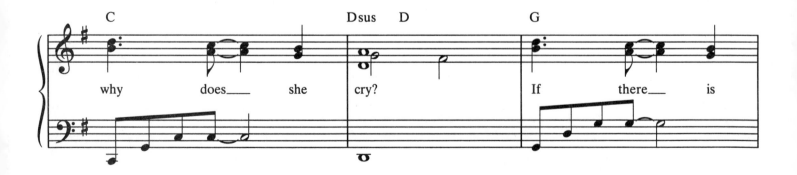

Em noth - ing___ **C** miss - ing in her life, why do tears **D7** come___ at night?

Chorus:

G *mf* "She's so luck - y, **Em** she's a star." But she **C** cry, cry, cries in her

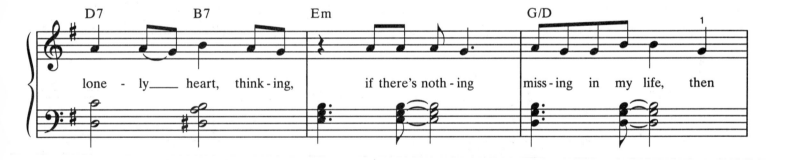

D7 lone - ly___ heart, think - ing, **B7** **Em** if there's noth - ing **G/D** miss - ing in my life, then

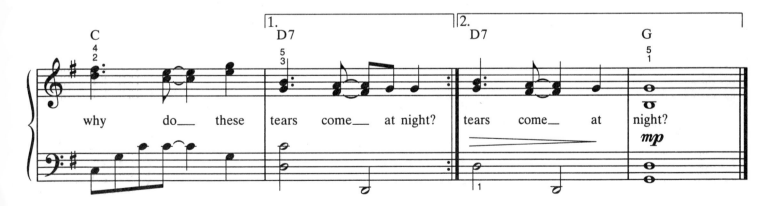

C why do___ these **1. D7** tears come___ at night? **2. D7** tears come___ at **G** night? *mp*

MY EVERYTHING

Words and Music by
ARNTHOR BIRGISSON, ANDERS SVEN BAGGE,
NICK LACHEY and ANDREW LACHEY
Arranged by DAN COATES

Slowly, with expression
Verse:

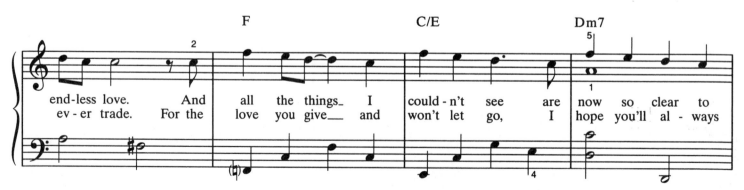

My Everything - 4 - 1

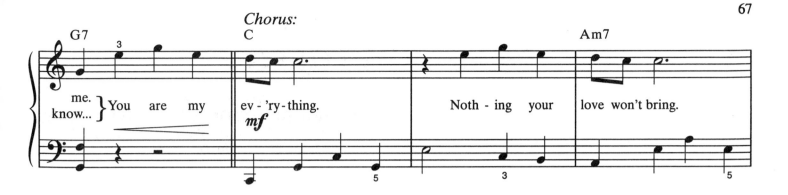

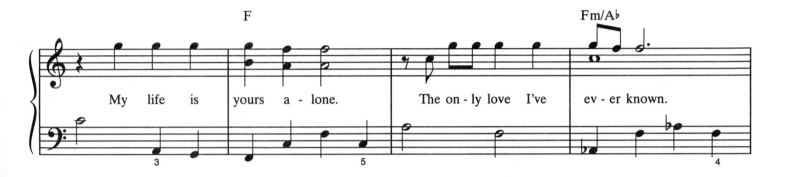

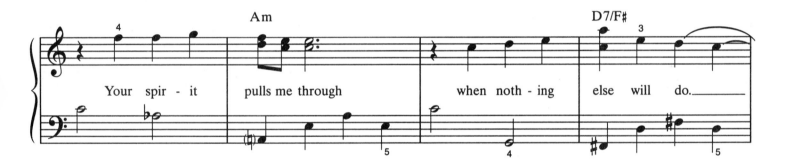

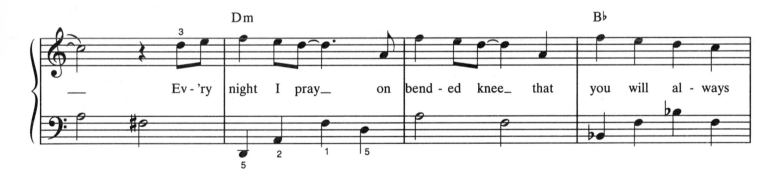

Chorus:

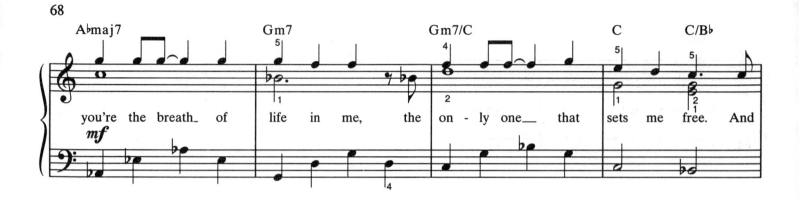

you're the breath_ of life in me, the on-ly one__ that sets me free. And

you have made_ my soul com-plete for all time. You are my

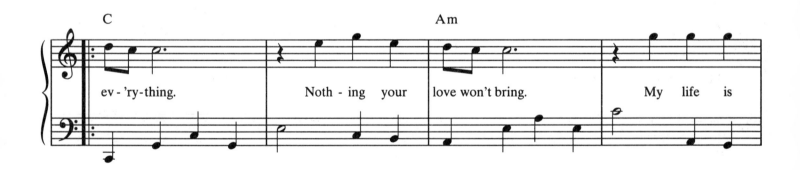

ev-'ry-thing. Noth-ing your love won't bring. My life is

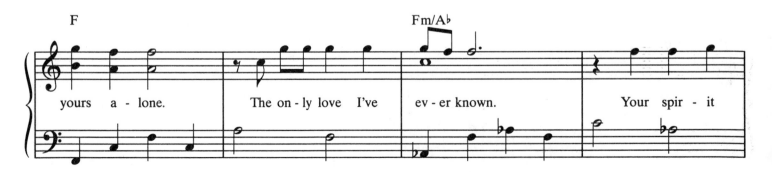

yours a-lone. The on-ly love I've ev-er known. Your spir-it

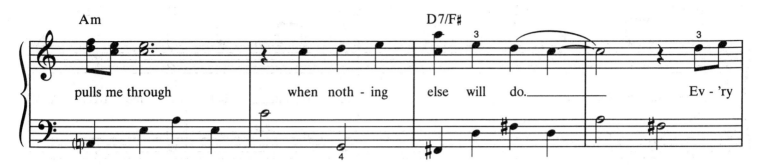

pulls me through   when noth - ing   else will do._____   Ev - 'ry

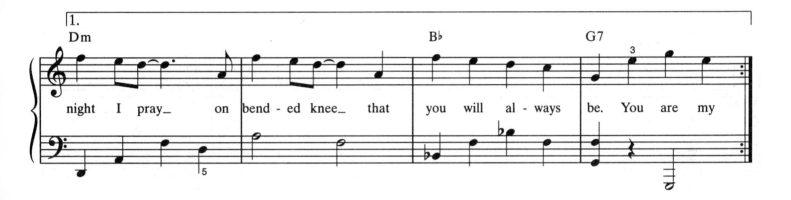

1.
night I pray___   on bend - ed knee___ that   you will al - ways   be. You are my

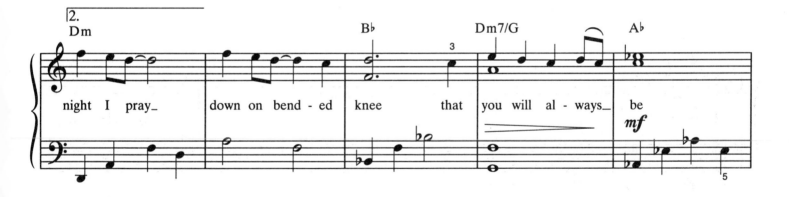

2.
night I pray___   down on bend - ed   knee   that you will al - ways___   be

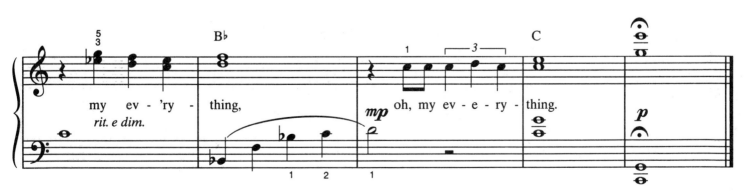

my ev - 'ry -   thing,   oh, my ev - e - ry - thing.
rit. e dim.

NEED TO BE NEXT TO YOU

Words and Music by
DIANE WARREN
Arranged by DAN COATES

Slowly (♩ = 88)

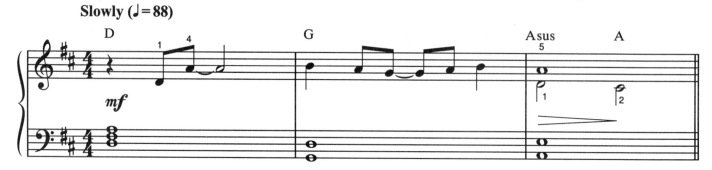

Verse:

1. Been run - ning from these feel - ings for so long,__ tell - ing my heart I did - n't need
2. Right here with you is right where I be - long.__ I'll lose my mind if I can't see

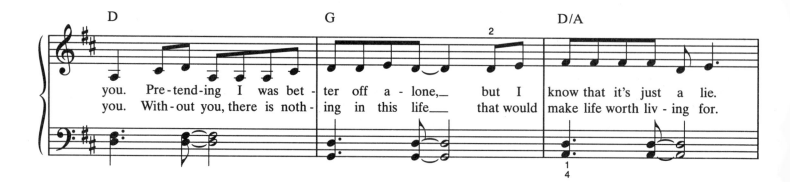

you. Pre - tend-ing I was bet - ter off a - lone,__ but I know that it's just a lie.
you. With - out you, there is noth - ing in this life__ that would make life worth liv - ing for.

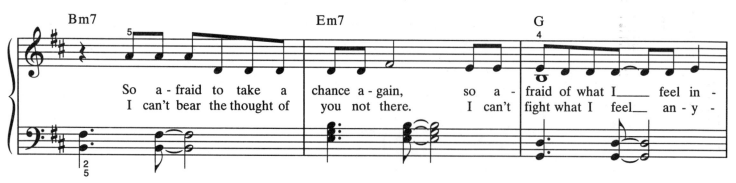

So a - fraid to take a chance a - gain, so a - fraid of what I____ feel in -
I can't bear the thought of you not there. I can't fight what I feel__ an - y -

Chorus:

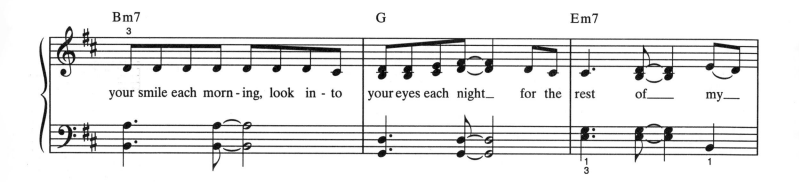

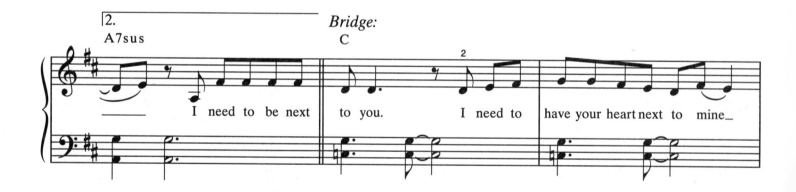

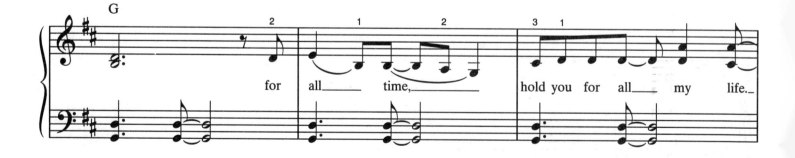

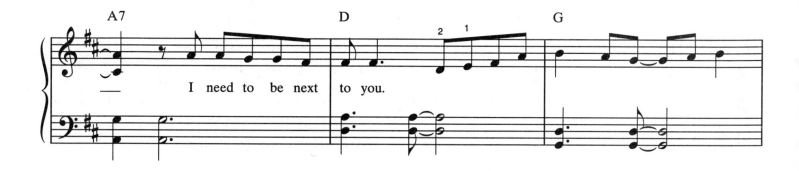

SHAPE OF MY HEART

Words and Music by
MAX MARTIN, RAMI
and LISA MISKOVSKY
Arranged by DAN COATES

Moderately slow (♩ = 96)

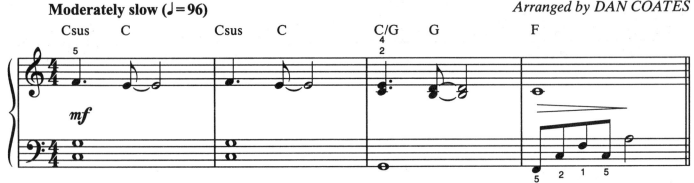

Verse:

1. Ba - by,___ please try___ to for - give me.___
2. Sad - ness is beau - ti - ful.___ Lone - li - ness is

trag - i - cal.___ So Stay here,___ don't put out the___ glow.
help me,___ I can't win this___ war.

Hold me now,___ don't both -
Touch me now,___ don't both -

Shape of My Heart - 4 - 1

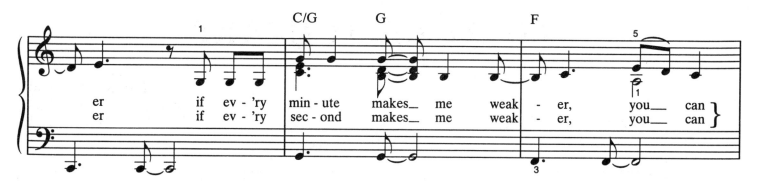

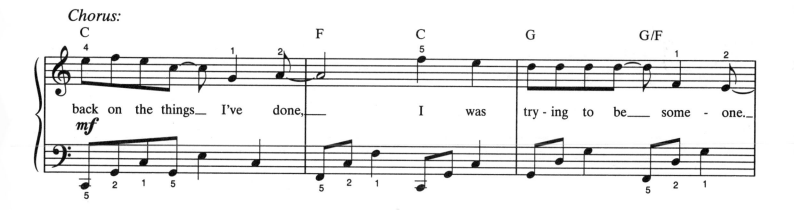

show you___ the shape of___ my heart.

Bridge:

shape of___ my heart. I'm here with my con - fes - sion,

mp

got noth-ing to hide___ no more.___ I don't know where___ to

start but to show you___ the shape of___ my

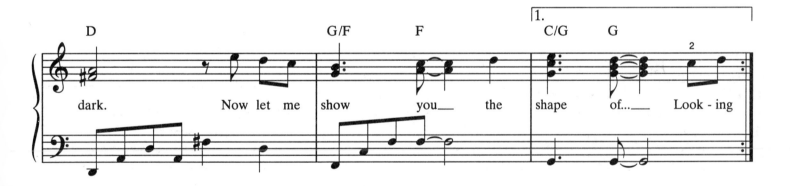

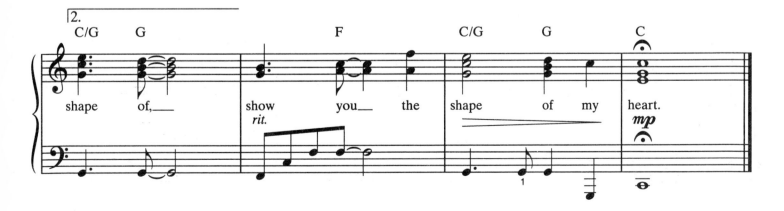

STRONGER

Words and Music by
MAX MARTIN and RAMI
Arranged by DAN COATES

Moderately, with a strong beat (♩ = 108)

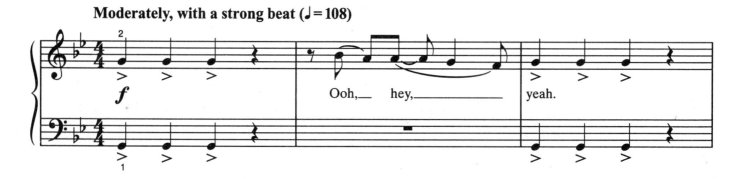

Ooh,— hey,———— yeah.

1. Hush, just stop.
strong - er

There's noth - ing you can
than I ev - er thought that

do or say.
I could be.

Ba - by,— I've had e - nough.
Ba - by,— I used to go with the

I'm not your prop - er - ty as
flow, did - n't real - ly

from to - day,
care 'bout me.

ba - by.—

Stronger - 4 - 1

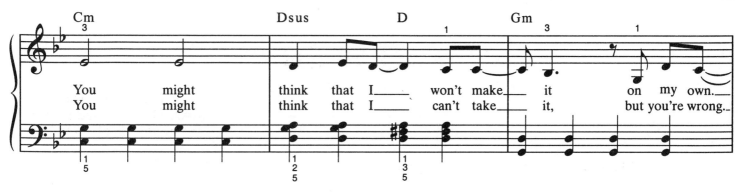

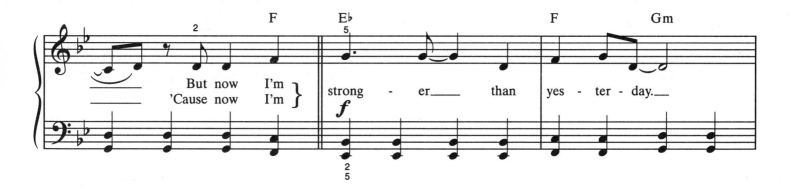

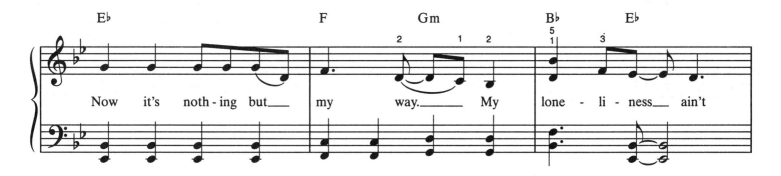

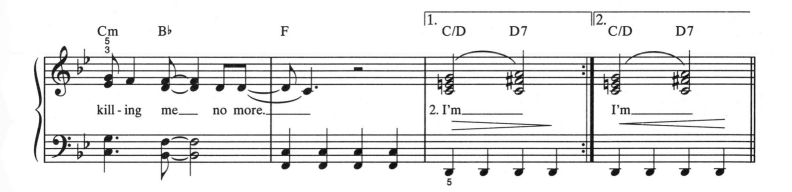

Stronger - 4 - 2

Oh, yeah.___ Here I go, on my own. I don't

need no-bod-y, bet-ter off a-lone. Here I go,___ on my own now.

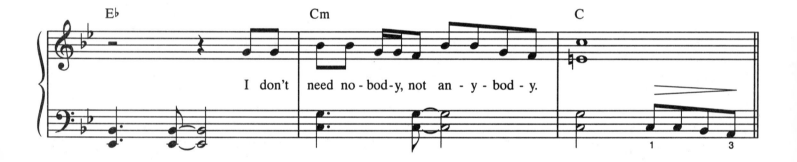

I don't need no-bod-y, not an-y-bod-y.

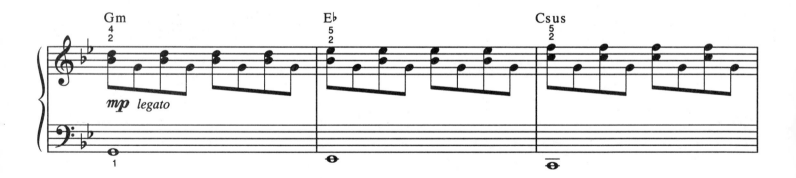

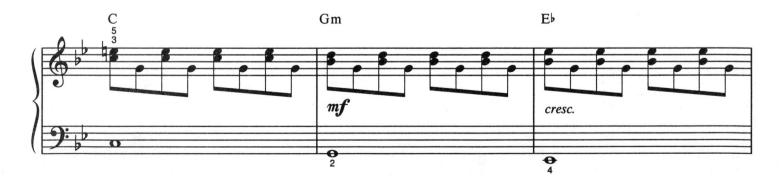

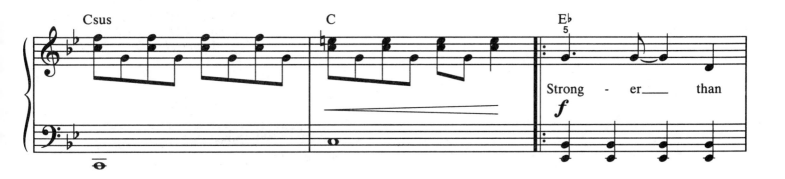

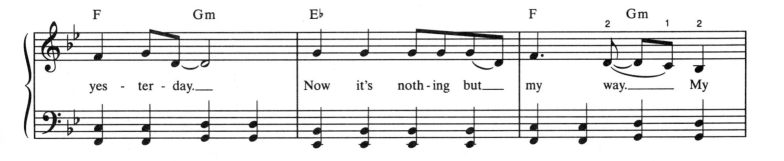

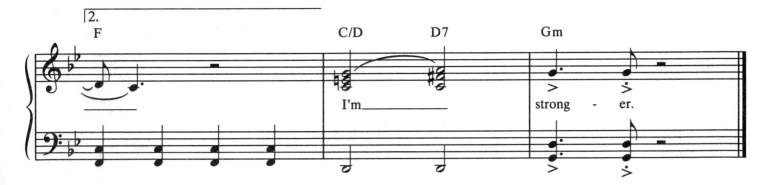

SHOW ME THE MEANING
OF BEING LONELY

Words and Music by
MAX MARTIN and HERBERT CRICHLOW
Arranged by DAN COATES

Moderately slow

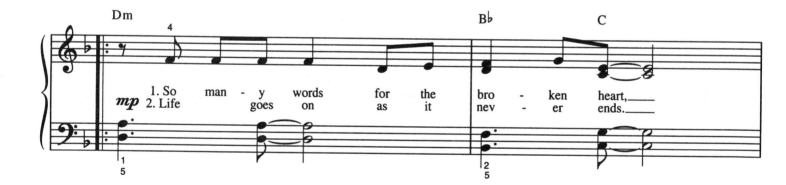

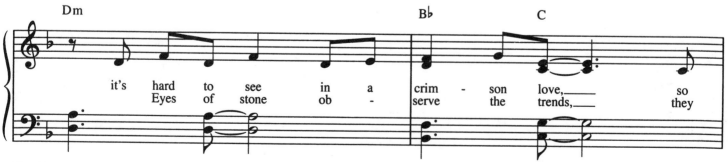

Show Me the Meaning of Being Lonely - 5 - 1

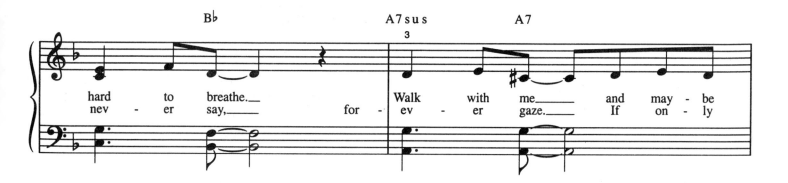

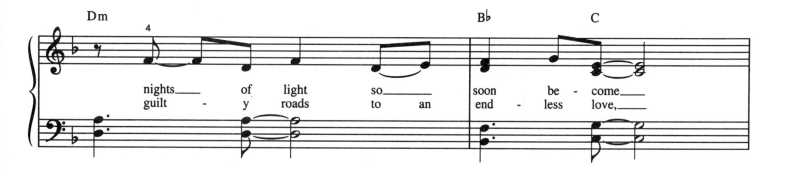

Show Me the Meaning of Being Lonely - 5 - 2

84

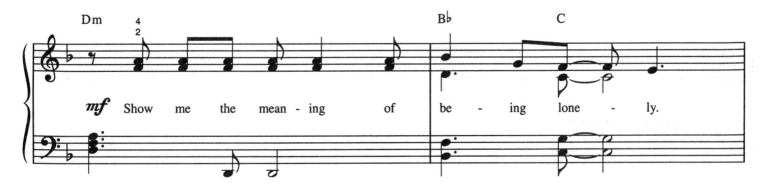

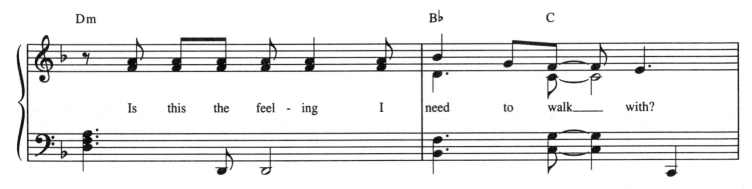

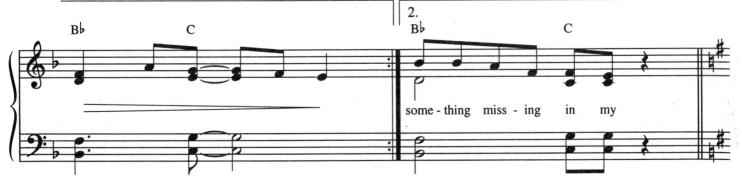

Show Me the Meaning of Being Lonely - 5 - 3

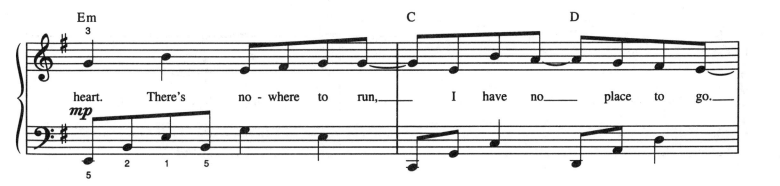

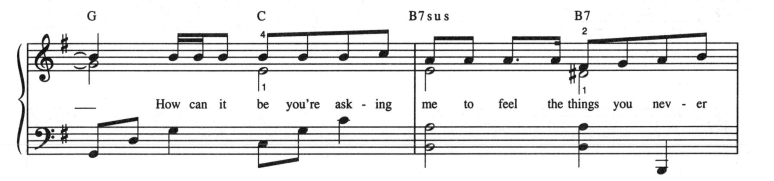

Show Me the Meaning of Being Lonely - 5 - 4

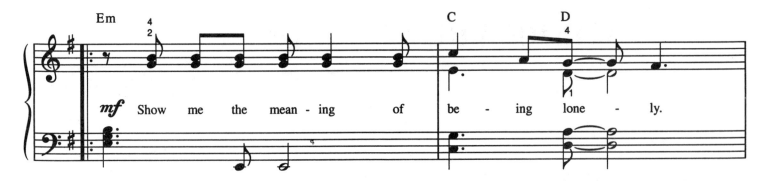

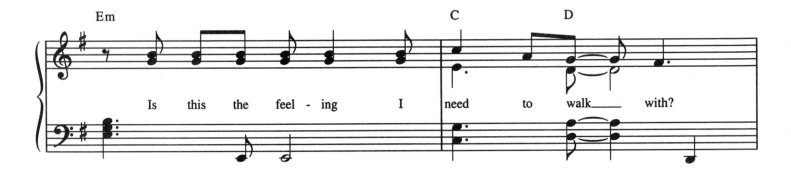

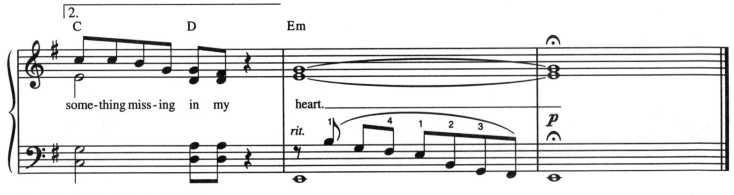

Show me the mean-ing of be-ing lone-ly.

Is this the feel-ing I need to walk____ with?

Tell me why I can't be there____ where you

are. There's some-thing miss-ing in my heart.

some-thing miss-ing in my heart.____

Show Me the Meaning of Being Lonely - 5 - 5

WHERE ARE YOU CHRISTMAS?

Words and Music by
JAMES HORNER, WILL JENNINGS
and MARIAH CAREY
Arranged by DAN COATES

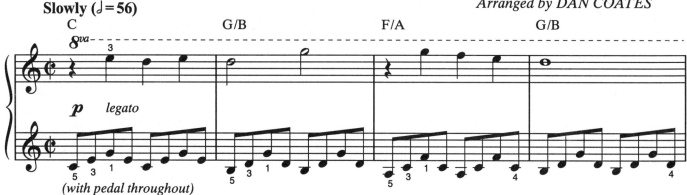

Verses 2 & 3:

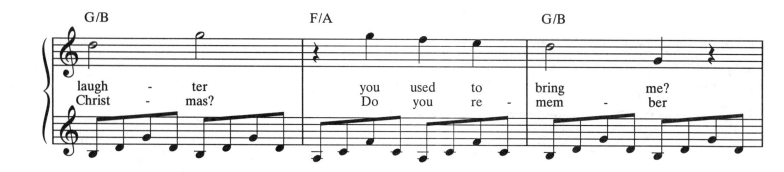

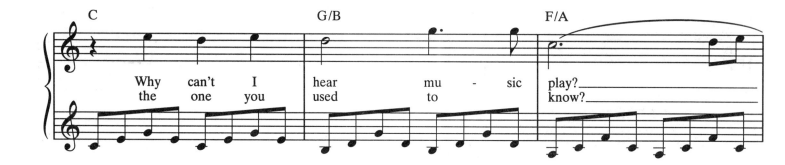

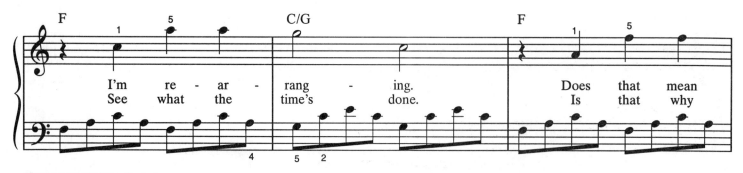

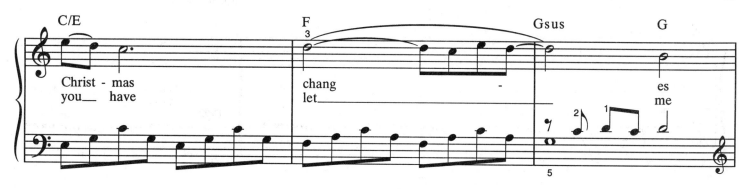

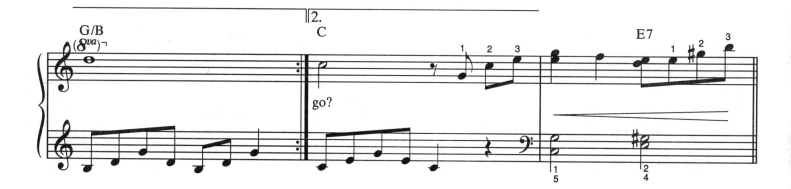

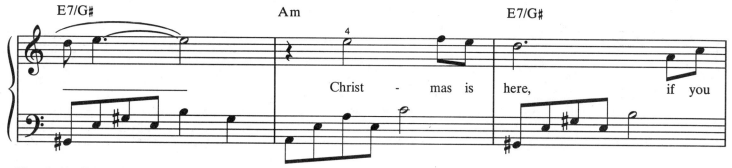

Where Are You Christmas? - 5 - 3

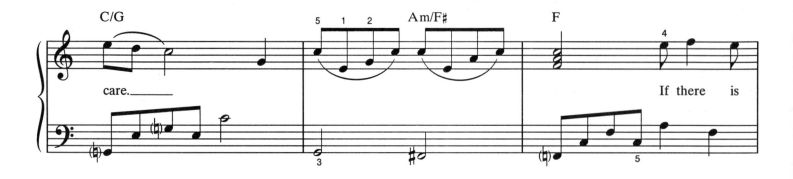

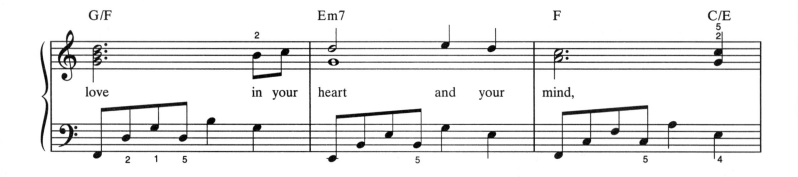

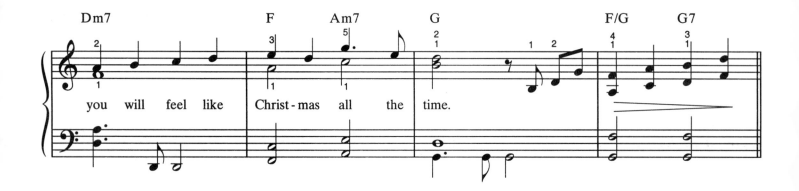

Verses 4 & 5:

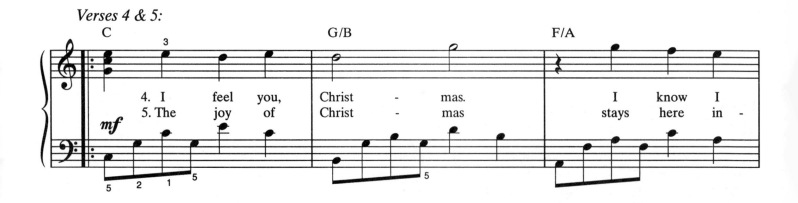

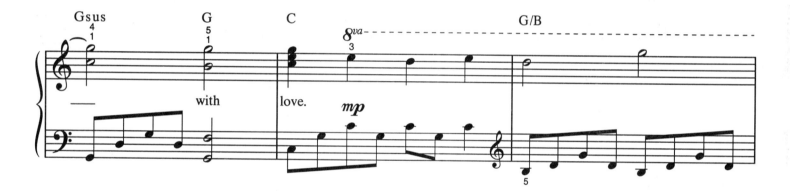

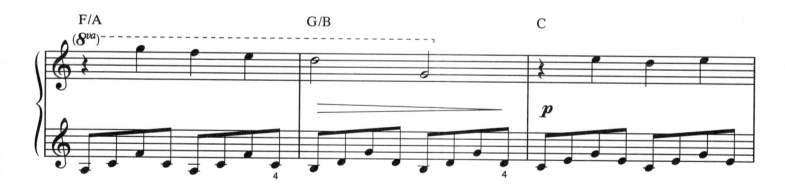

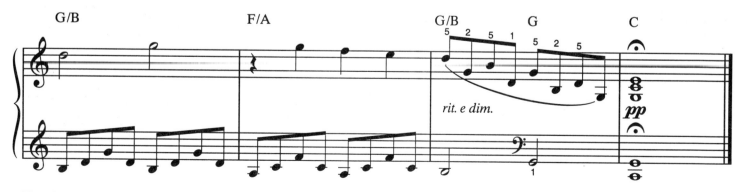

THANK YOU FOR LOVING ME

Words and Music by
JON BON JOVI and RICHIE SAMBORA
Arranged by DAN COATES

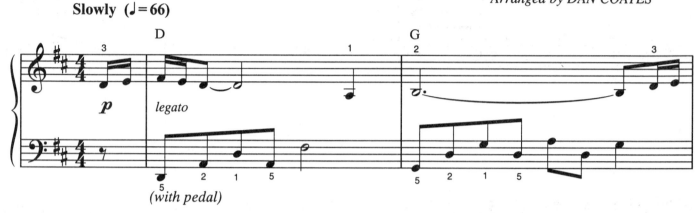

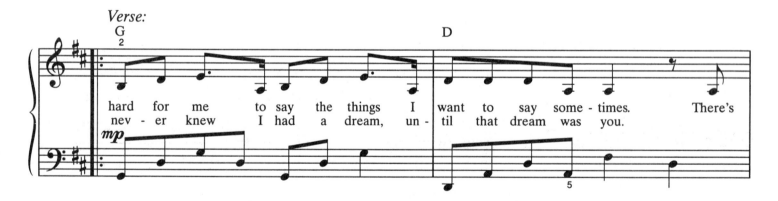

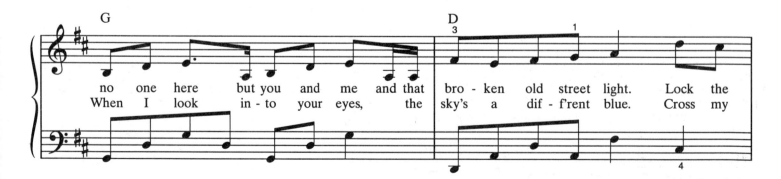

Thank You for Loving Me - 4 - 1

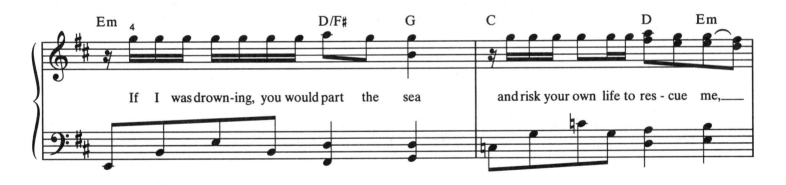

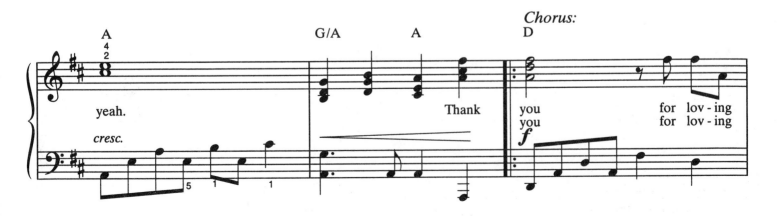

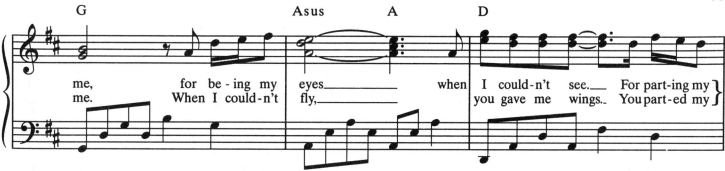

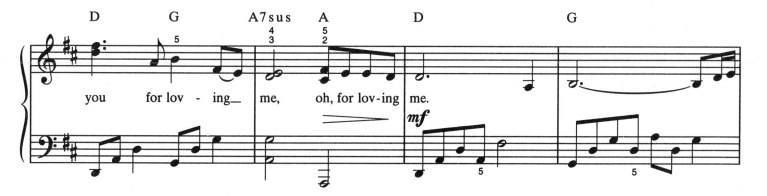

Thank You for Loving Me - 4 - 4

THAT'S THE WAY IT IS

Words and Music by
MAX MARTIN, KRISTIAN LUNDIN
and ANDREAS CARLSSON
Arranged by DAN COATES

Moderately slow, with a beat

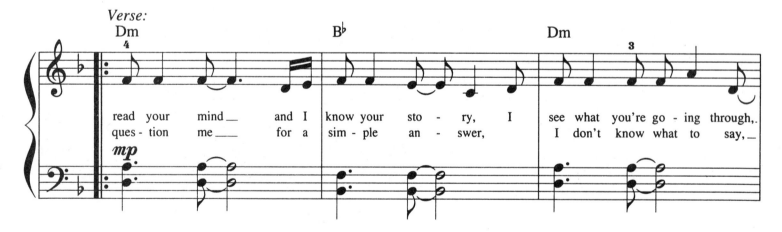

Verse:

read your mind___ and I know your sto - ry, I see what you're go - ing through,___
ques - tion me___ for a sim - ple an - swer, I don't know what to say,___

___ yeah.___ It's an up - hill climb___ and I'm feel - ing sor - ry,___ but I
___ no.___ But it's plain to see,___ if you stick to - geth - er,

That's the Way It Is - 4 - 1

know it will come to you, ___ yeah. ___ } Don't sur - ren - der, ___ 'cause
you're gon - na find the way, ___ yeah. ___

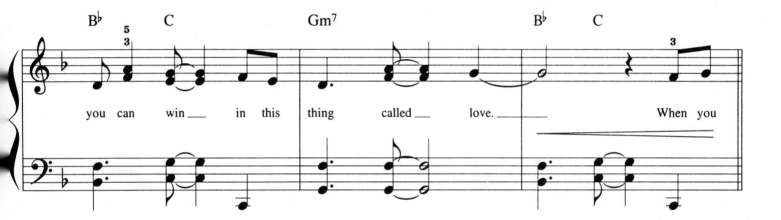

you can win ___ in this thing called ___ love. ___ When you

Chorus:

want it the most, ___ there's no eas - y way out. ___ When you're read - y to go ___ and your heart's

___ left in doubt, ___ don't give up on your faith; ___ love comes to those ___ who be - lieve ___

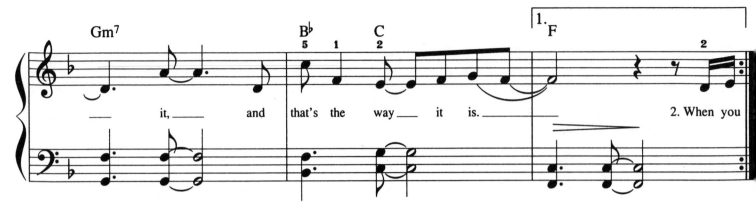

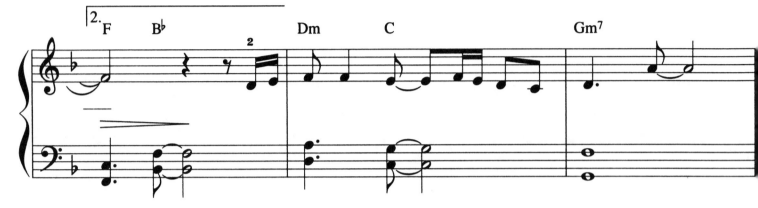

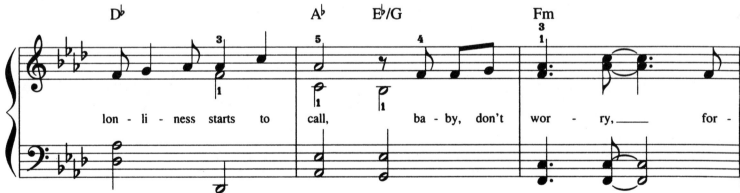

That's the Way It Is - 4 - 3

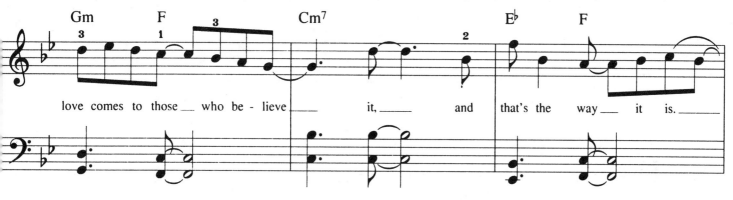

That's the Way It Is - 4 - 4

THIS I PROMISE YOU

Words and Music by
RICHARD MARX
Arranged by DAN COATES

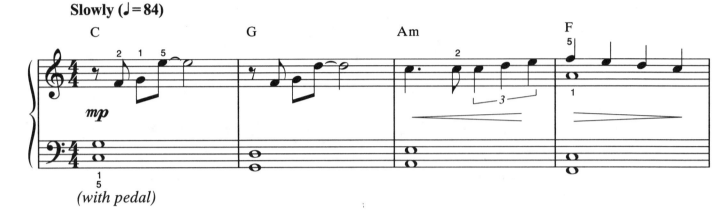

(with pedal)

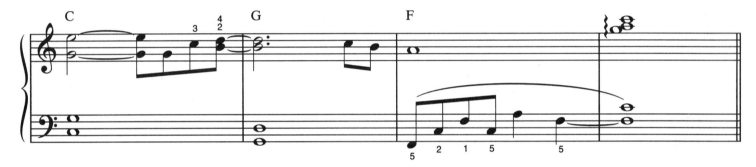

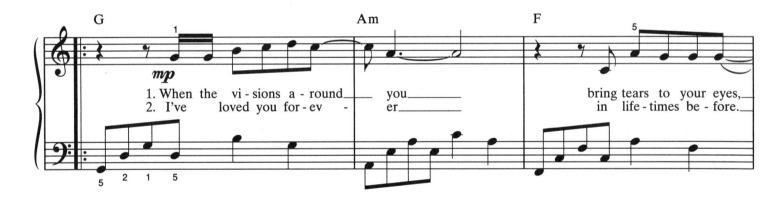

1. When the vi-sions a-round_____ you_____ bring tears to your eyes,_____
2. I've loved you for-ev - er_____ in life-times be-fore._____

and all that sur-rounds_____ you
And I prom-ise you, nev - er

This I Promise You - 4 - 1

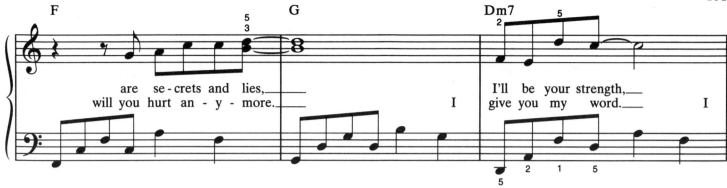

F   G   Dm7

are se‑crets and lies,_____
will you hurt an‑y‑more._____   I

I'll be your strength,_____
give you my word._____   I

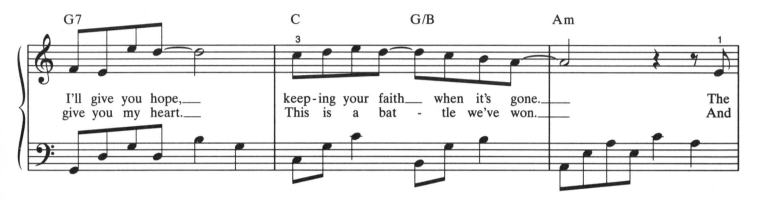

G7   C   G/B   Am

I'll give you hope,_____
give you my heart._____

keep‑ing your faith_____ when it's gone._____
This is a bat‑tle we've won._____   The
And

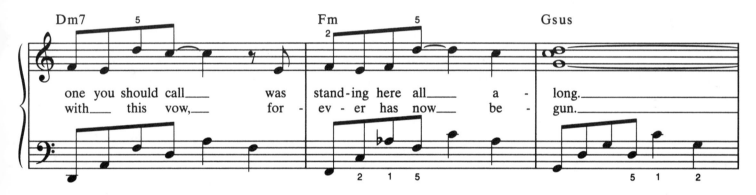

Dm7   Fm   Gsus

one you should call_____ was
with_____ this vow,_____ for‑

stand‑ing here all_____ a‑
ev‑er has now_____ be‑

long._____
gun._____

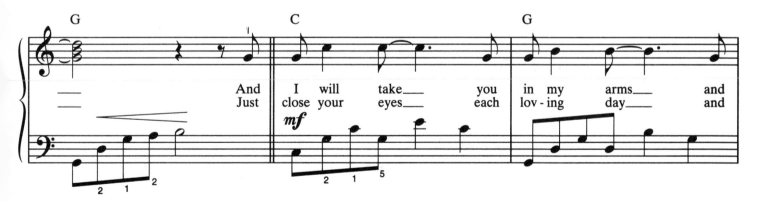

G   C   G

_____
_____   Just

And   I will take_____ you
close your eyes_____ each

in my arms_____ and
lov‑ing day_____ and

mf

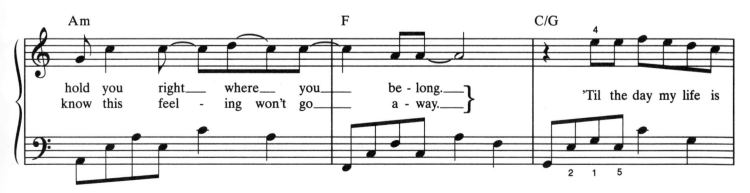

Am   F   C/G

hold you right_____ where_____ you_____ be‑long._____
know this feel‑ing won't go_____ a‑way._____

'Til the day my life is

This I Promise You - 4 - 2

through, this I prom - ise you.　　　　This I prom - ise you.

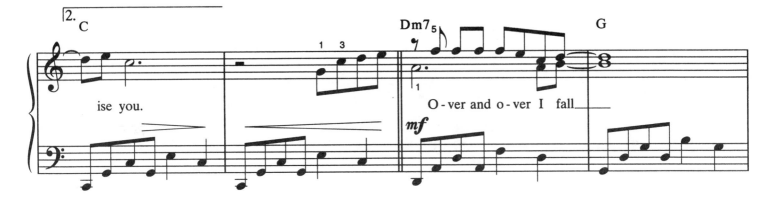

ise you.　　　　O - ver and o - ver I fall

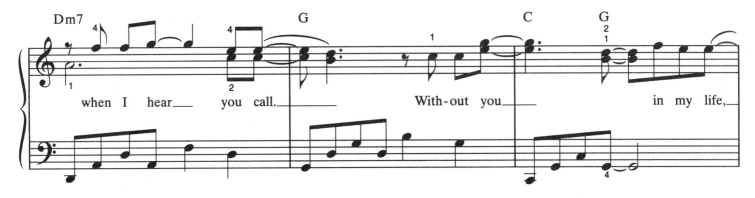

when I hear___ you call.___　With - out you___　in my life,

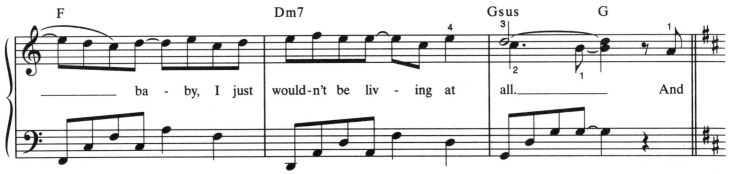

_____ ba - by, I just would-n't be liv - ing at　all._____　And

I will take___ you in my arms___ and hold you right___ where_ you
close your eyes___ each lov-ing day___ and know this feel - ing won't go_

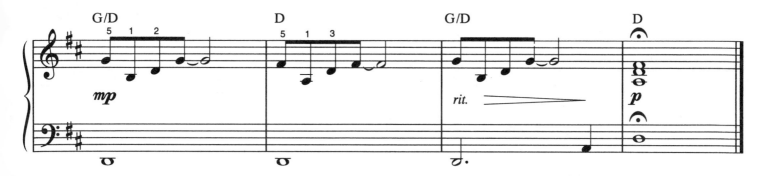

This I Promise You - 4 - 4

WIN

Words and Music by
BRIAN McNIGHT and BRANDON BARNES
Arranged by DAN COATES

Moderately slow ($\lozenge$ = 64)

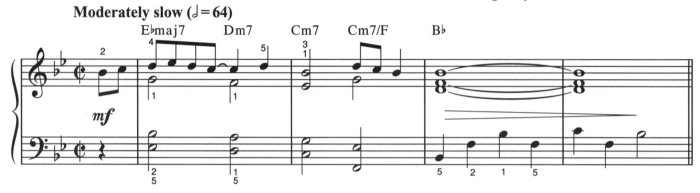

Verse:

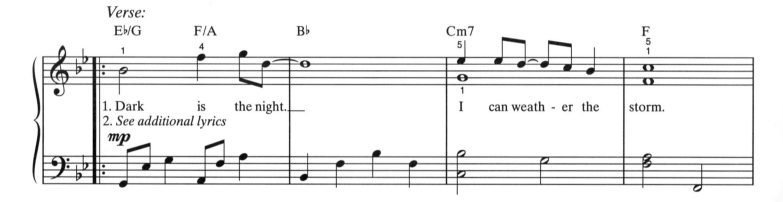

1. Dark is the night.___ I can weath-er the storm.
2. *See additional lyrics*

Nev-er say die.___ I've been down this road___ be-fore. I'll nev-er

quit, I'll nev-er break down. See, I

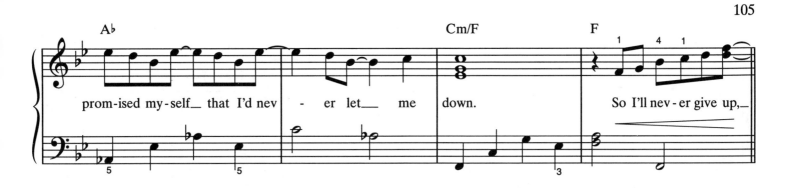

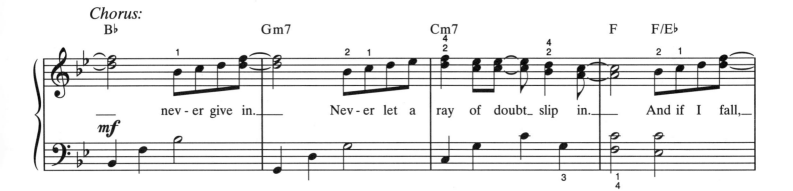

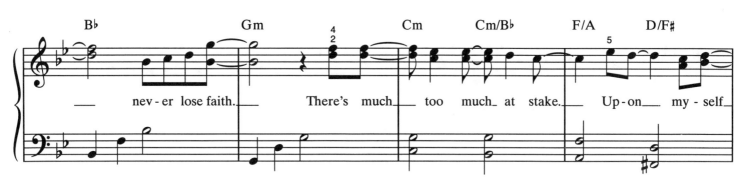

Win - 5 - 2

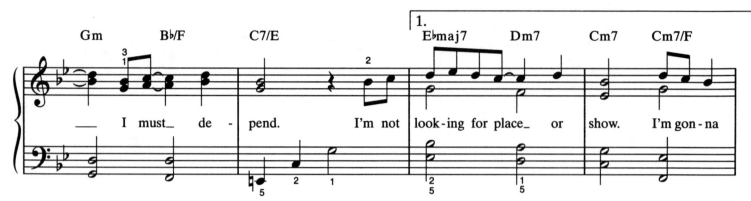

I must— de - pend. I'm not look-ing for place_ or show. I'm gon-na

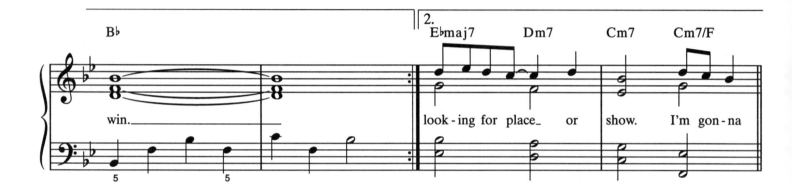

win._____ look-ing for place_ or show. I'm gon-na

Bridge:

win. When it's all___ said_ and_ done,_____ my "once in a

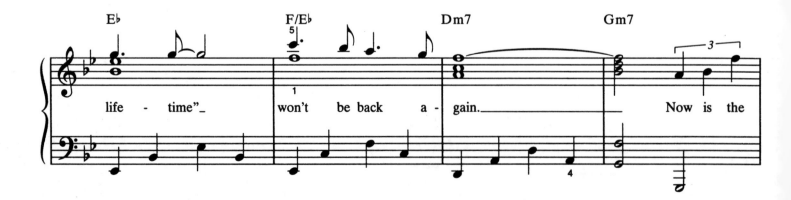

life - time"_ won't be back a - gain._____ Now is the

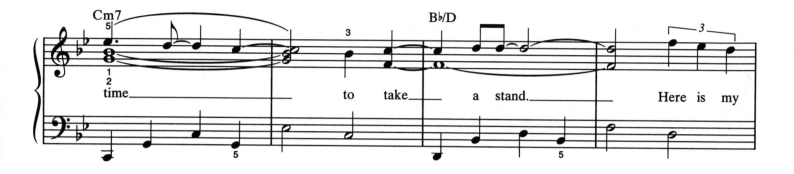

nev - er lose faith. There's much too much at stake. Up - on my - self

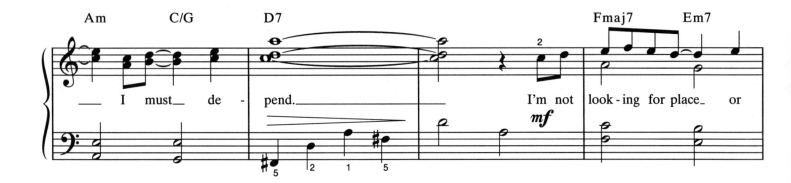

I must de - pend. I'm not look-ing for place or

mf

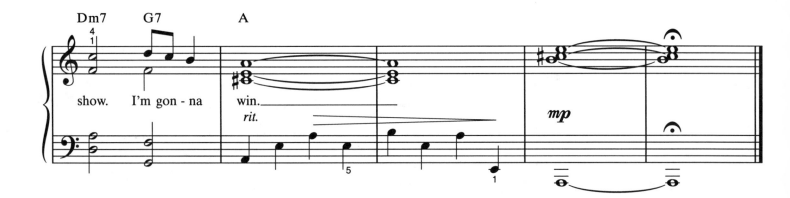

show. I'm gon - na win.

rit. *mp*

Verse 2:
No stopping now,
There's still a ways to go.
Some way, somehow,
Whatever it takes, I know
I'll never quit.
I'll never go down.
I'll make sure they remember my name
A hundred years from now.
(To Chorus:)